D1143014

JULIUS CAESAR

JULIUS CAESAR

Edited by Arthur E. Meikle

Principal English Master,
Hutchesons' Boys' Grammar School, Glasgow

Illustrated by Colin Winslow

LONDON   EDWARD ARNOLD (PUBLISHERS) LTD

© Arthur Meikle
First published 1964
Reprinted 1965 (twice), 1969, 1970, 1971, 1973, 1977, 1979

ISBN: 0 7131 1129 1

THE KENNET SHAKESPEARE

Hamlet
Macbeth
Julius Caesar
Richard II
As You Like It
Romeo and Juliet
Henry IV, Part I
Twelfth Night
Henry V
The Tempest
The Merchant of Venice
A Midsummer Night's Dream

ACKNOWLEDGEMENTS

Julius Caesar was first published in the First Folio, the first collected edition of Shakespeare's works, which appeared in 1623. The text here used is based upon that of Professor Peter Alexander, published by Collins. The Arden edition (T. S. Dorsch) and the New Cambridge (J. Dover Wilson) have also been consulted.

Of the multitude of valuable critical works available, the following have been especially helpful:

Peter Alexander, *Shakespeare's Life and Art*
Maurice Charney, *Shakespeare's Roman Plays*
Harley Granville-Barker, *Prefaces to Shakespeare*
G. B. Harrison, *Introducing Shakespeare*
Hilda Hulme, *Explorations in Shakespeare's Language*
G. Wilson Knight, *Principles of Shakespearian Production*
E. F. C. Ludowyk, *Understanding Shakespeare*
M. W. MacCallum, *Shakespeare's Roman Plays*
J. S. Manifold, *The Music in English Drama*
John Palmer, *The Political Characters of Shakespeare*
Irving Ribner, *Patterns in Shakespearian Tragedy*

I am also very grateful to Bernard Harris for directing me to published works on *Julius Caesar*; to John Nevinson for advice on illustrations; and to the Stratford Shakespearian Festival, Stratford, Ontario, for permission to base the drawing on p. 90 on one of their productions.

play on word of metal
mettle

INTRODUCTION

This play is about a political assassination and its consequences. But that bare statement gives little idea of the play's
richness. A great work is packed with significance, not all
consciously put there by the writer. Being a genius, he
intuitively penetrates to aspects of personality and fundamental truths which lesser mortals must laboriously discover
and ponder over. Therefore this play can be interpreted in
many ways which may all be valid, and at different times
some of these will be more relevant than others. We may say,
however, that there are two main themes, sometimes emerging
separately, and sometimes interwoven—one personal, one
political. The personal theme is the story of a man who sought
good ends by bad means; the political theme is the conflict
between two ideologies—dictatorship and republicanism.
These themes are of lasting interest and importance, and so
although the events of the play happened in Rome forty-four
years before the birth of Christ, and were recreated by a
dramatist writing in England in 1599, the play is still
relevant today, in any part of the world.

Shakespeare (1564–1616) did not invent the plot. Like
many of the greatest writers from ancient Greece onwards,
he relied not on ingenuity of plot invention but on his treatment of an existing and frequently familiar story. The story
of Julius Caesar was a favourite with the Elizabethans. The
version that Shakespeare used was based on a translation by
Sir Thomas North of a book by Plutarch, a Greek writer of
the first century A.D., who wrote the lives of celebrated
Greeks and Romans. Shakespeare made a close study of his
lives of Brutus, Caesar, and Antony, and soaked himself
thoroughly in the atmosphere of Rome in their age. In

writing *Julius Caesar* he drew very closely on Plutarch (or North) at some times, and at other times made changes to suit his own conception of the dramatic situation and the characters. He knew, for example, how Brutus and Antony spoke, and followed their styles in the speeches he wrote for them, but the all-important funeral orations are entirely his own composition. Casca too is Shakespeare's creation.

No attempt has been made in this edition to keep Shakespeare's punctuation. It is only misleading to anyone who has not made a special study of it. If the student reads the lines according to the punctuation given here he will generally find that the sense of the speech emerges, even if individual words and phrases are obscure.

Our picture gives a good idea of the opening scene of the play as originally produced at the Globe Theatre in September, 1599. The costumes are basically Elizabethan with a few Roman touches—such as the togas of Flavius and Marullus.

PRINCIPAL CHARACTERS
[in Order of Speaking]

FLAVIUS, a Tribune
MARULLUS, a Tribune
JULIUS CAESAR
CASCA, a Conspirator
CALPHURNIA, Caesar's wife
MARK ANTONY, Triumvir after the death of Caesar
A Soothsayer
MARCUS BRUTUS, a Conspirator
CAIUS CASSIUS, a Conspirator
CICERO, a Senator
CINNA, a Conspirator
LUCIUS, Brutus' servant
DECIUS BRUTUS, a Conspirator
METELLUS CIMBER, a Conspirator
TREBONIUS, a Conspirator
PORTIA, Brutus' wife
CAIUS LIGARIUS, a Conspirator
PUBLIUS, a Senator
ARTEMIDORUS, a Sophist
POPILIUS LENA, a Senator
CINNA, a Poet
OCTAVIUS CAESAR, Triumvir after the death of Caesar
MARCUS AEMILIUS LEPIDUS, Triumvir after the death of Caesar
LUCILIUS, an Officer in the Conspirators' army
PINDARUS, Cassius' servant
A Poet
MESSALA, an Officer in the Conspirators' army
TITINIUS, an Officer in the Conspirators' army
VARRO, a Soldier attached to Brutus
The Ghost of Julius Caesar
CLAUDIUS, a Soldier attached to Brutus
Young CATO, an Officer in the Conspirators' army
CLITUS, an Officer attached to Brutus
DARDANIUS, an Officer attached to Brutus
VOLUMNIUS, an Officer attached to Brutus
STRATO, an Officer attached to Brutus
A Carpenter, a Cobbler, and other Citizens; Servants; Senators;
  Guards; Attendants

[11]

JULIUS CAESAR

Rome. A street

In a modern production the curtain rises on a street scene in Rome,
44 B.C. Trumpets are heard off stage. The stage is full of working-
class people, out enjoying themselves, talking and shouting. All are
in high spirits, and are in gay clothes, some wearing garlands on
their heads. There is a great deal of movement, and good-natured
jostling. Two impressive figures wearing togas break through the
crowd. These two are highly important officials called tribunes.
They are by no means festive—they are looking angry, and try to
avoid being touched by the merrymakers. One of them, Flavius,
barks at the people, who quieten down just enough to let him be
heard, but some go on joking among themselves, and those who
crowd round to hear the conversation between the tribunes and
the Second Commoner greet their friend's sallies with appreciative
guffaws, thus encouraging his increasingly successful efforts to
goad the great men. About line 32 the noise subsides, and Marullus'
big speech is heard in silence from line 35, the crowd becoming
more and more sober until about 20 lines later they are shamefaced.

3 *mechanical*   tradesmen or labourers, manual workers. Today we
   would more naturally use a noun, though Shakespeare's word is
   an adjective.

4–5 *the sign Of your profession.*   This is not a distinctive badge or
   costume, but merely working clothes or implements, as in line 7.

11 *cobbler.*   The word is ambiguous, either (a) a shoemaker, or
   (b) an unskilled worker. Marullus takes the latter meaning,
   guided to it by *in respect of* (having regard to) *a fine workman.*

14 The Second Commoner is enjoying the opportunity of baiting
   his betters. The pun is weakened when written down; when
   spoken, 'soles' is indistinguishable from 'souls', and the speaker,
   with his reference to *a safe conscience*, and no doubt a pious
   expression and intonation, has successfully misled Marullus
   again.

15 *naughty*   worth naught, therefore good for nothing; stronger
   than in modern English.

17 *be not out*   don't be angry.

18 *if you be out*   if you should be out at heel. The man juggles
   neatly with two meanings of one phrase.

22 Flavius, being less incensed than Marullus, sees through the
   deliberate mystification.

[12]

JULIUS CAESAR

ACT ONE

SCENE ONE

Enter FLAVIUS, MARULLUS, *and* Commoners

FLAVIUS: Hence! home, you idle creatures, get you home.
Is this a holiday? What, know you not,
Being mechanical, you ought not walk
Upon a labouring day without the sign
Of your profession? Speak, what trade art thou? 5

FIRST COMMONER: Why, sir, a carpenter.

MARULLUS: Where is thy leather apron and thy rule?
What dost thou with thy best apparel on?
You, sir, what trade are you?

SECOND COMMONER: Truly, sir, in respect of a fine workman, I 10
am but, as you would say, a cobbler.

MARULLUS: But what trade art thou? Answer me directly.

SECOND COMMONER: A trade, sir, that I hope I may use with a
safe conscience; which is, indeed, sir, a mender of bad soles.

MARULLUS: What trade, thou knave? Thou naughty knave, 15
what trade?

SECOND COMMONER: Nay, I beseech you, sir, be not out with
me; yet, if you be out, sir, I can mend you.

MARULLUS: What meanest thou by that? Mend me, thou
saucy fellow? 20

SECOND COMMONER: Why, sir, cobble you.

FLAVIUS: Thou art a cobbler, art thou?

25 This is another pun. 'With all' makes sense; so does 'withal', meaning 'at the same time'. Whichever way it is printed, the hearer is left to decide on the meaning. People today tend to regard the pun as a weak form of humour, and the usual reaction to a pun is a groan. In Shakespeare's day any display of verbal ingenuity was appreciated, and puns were greeted with delight. But though frequently used for fun, they were approved of also in serious contexts, and were felt to heighten the expression of any emotion.

26 *recover*   restore to health, or put on a new cover.

26–7 *as fine a man as ever wore shoes*—a proverbial expression. *neat*   ox.

32 There could be another sounding of trumpets at the word 'work'. Then the Second Commoner drops his bantering style and speaks seriously.

33 *triumph*.   This is a technical term for a high ceremonial procession accorded to a general for a major victory. Caesar entered Rome in triumph after the battle of Munda in 45 B.C., in which he defeated the sons of Pompey the Great.

34 Note the fluent impassioned poetry of this speech in contrast to the homely prose of the preceding conversation; note too that it was sparked off by the first mention of the name of Caesar.

35 *tributaries*   conquered chiefs who would pay tribute, annual taxes, on being restored to their positions.

36 *captive bonds*   the bonds, or chains, of prisoners.

39 *Pompey*.   Pompey the Great had been one of the rulers of Rome, but was later defeated by Caesar, his former friend and partner.

44 *pass the streets*   pass through the streets.

47 *her*.   Unusual. The Romans spoke of 'Father Tiber'.

48 *replication*   reverberation, derived from 'reply'.

49 *concave*   hollowed out by the swift stream, therefore likely to produce echoes.

49–54 The series of questions is delivered in a rising tone till the final explosion of the dramatic short line.

51 *cull*   pick. Pick this day for a holiday. But the word is frequently associated with flowers, and so leads naturally to the next line.

53 *That*   in the way of him that comes. *That* is a relative pronoun, antecedent *his*. *Pompey's blood*.   Both Pompey and his elder son had died in their struggle against Caesar, Pompey himself in 48 B.C. and the son in 45 B.C., just after Munda.

56 *intermit*   stop, as though putting a barrier in its way.

57 *light*   alight, come down.

SECOND COMMONER: Truly, sir, all that I live by is with the
awl. I meddle with no tradesman's matters, nor women's
matters, but with awl. I am, indeed, sir, a surgeon to old   25
shoes; when they are in great danger I recover them. As
proper men as ever trod upon neat's leather have gone upon
my handiwork.

FLAVIUS: But wherefore art not in thy shop to-day?
Why dost thou lead these men about the streets?   30

SECOND COMMONER: Truly, sir, to wear out their shoes, to get
myself into more work. But indeed, sir, we make holiday
to see Caesar, and to rejoice in his triumph.

MARULLUS: Wherefore rejoice? What conquest brings he
home?
What tributaries follow him to Rome,   35
To grace in captive bonds his chariot wheels?
You blocks, you stones, you worse than senseless things!
O you hard hearts, you cruel men of Rome,
Knew you not Pompey? Many a time and oft
Have you climbed up to walls and battlements,   40
To towers and windows, yea, to chimney-tops,
Your infants in your arms, and there have sat
The live-long day, with patient expectation,
To see great Pompey pass the streets of Rome.
And when you saw his chariot but appear,   45
Have you not made an universal shout,
That Tiber trembled underneath her banks
To hear the replication of your sounds
Made in her concave shores?
And do you now put on your best attire?   50
And do you now cull out a holiday?
And do you now strew flowers in his way
That comes in triumph over Pompey's blood?
Be gone!
Run to your houses, fall upon your knees,   55
Pray to the gods to intermit the plague
That needs must light on this ingratitude.

58–67 Flavius again speaks more moderately, yet as the chastened people depart at line 63 he does not display much sympathy for them.

63 *whe'r* whether. *metal* or 'mettle', spirit. Shakespeare uses both spellings without distinction, and as there is no difference in sound, and both meanings make good sense, both are valid.

65 *Capitol* temple of Jupiter.

67 *ceremonies* ceremonial decorations.

68 Now that his indignation has had an outlet in his long speech, Marullus shows more caution than Flavius.

69 *the feast of Lupercal.* The Lupercalia, a festival of purification and fertility, was a sacred occasion. Marullus has no desire to be accused of tampering with decorations put up in honour of a god. Shakespeare devised this complication by making Caesar's triumph coincide with the Lupercalia; in fact the triumph was four months earlier. If history and dramatic effect clash, history has to go.

71 *trophies* emblems such as banners, wreaths, floral displays, etc.

72 *the vulgar* the vulgus or plebs, the common people.

75 *pitch* the highest point of flight. A falconry term.

76 *Who.* The antecedent is *him.*

The opening scene should put us in the right frame of mind to enjoy the play, and give us enough information to arouse our interest in the story that is to be unfolded. If we pause now for a moment, what comes back to our minds?

(i) We have all the information we need regarding time and place—we are in Rome in the days of Julius Caesar. (ii) The situation is quite exciting: Caesar has won a great victory, and Rome is celebrating. (iii) There is some difference of opinion, however, concerning Caesar; the people are enthusiastic about him, but some superior Romans are not pleased with his success.

These things are obvious. Note in addition:

(i) We have been introduced to 'the crowd'. They are going to be very important in this play. Study them: as seen here they appear good-natured, fond of a laugh, ready with their devotion to a great national hero, quickly brought to heel by the impassioned speech of a superior. This speaker accuses them of fickleness. (ii) We have not been introduced yet to Caesar, but we have heard enough to know that his personality dominates Rome at this time.

[16]

FLAVIUS: Go, go, good countrymen, and for this fault
  Assemble all the poor men of your sort;
  Draw them to Tiber banks, and weep your tears   *60*
  Into the channel, till the lowest stream
  Do kiss the most exalted shores of all.
                      Exeunt all the Commoners
  See, whe'r their basest metal be not moved;
  They vanish tongue-tied in their guiltiness.
  Go you down that way towards the Capitol;   *65*
  This way will I. Disrobe the images,
  If you do find them decked with ceremonies.
MARULLUS: May we do so?
  You know it is the feast of Lupercal.
FLAVIUS: It is no matter; let no images   *70*
  Be hung with Caesar's trophies. I'll about,
  And drive away the vulgar from the streets;
  So do you too, where you perceive them thick.
  These growing feathers plucked from Caesar's wing
  Will make him fly an ordinary pitch,   *75*
  Who else would soar above the view of men
  And keep us all in servile fearfulness.   *Exeunt*

A public place

S.D. (means 'stage direction' throughout) *Flourish.* Flourishes, usually fairly brief signals announcing the approach of some important person or drawing attention to an important event, could be played on various instruments. This one must be on trumpets, which Shakespeare always used for persons of the very highest rank. Caesar can be given prominence by being carried on a litter. Everyone is gay, the nobility restrained but cheerful, the crowd much as we saw them at the beginning of the play, evidently recovered from the scolding of Marullus. He and Flavius, on the other hand, not mingling with the rest, look very surly. Among the crowd are several young men, stripped, like Antony, for running, and carrying leather thongs. Though not marching with military precision, the procession is orderly, following Caesar—a contrast to the confused rabble that shuffled off at 1.1.63.

1–9 In the Lupercalia childless women held out their hands hoping that the young men running about the streets would hit them with leather thongs and so cure their childlessness. These are Caesar's first words in the play. Do they suggest that Caesar is superstitious?

9–10 These are the first words of Antony. Is the compliment to Caesar fulsome?

12 The Soothsayer calls out in a startlingly high, piercing voice. He is old and small, easily bundled aside at line 24.

15 *press* crowd.

17 Note the imperious manner of Caesar, referring to himself in the third person. When he does this he is very conscious of his own importance, and is making sure that other people will not forget it.

18 *the ides of March* March 15.

19 In contrast to the Soothsayer with his highly charged tone, Brutus is quiet and matter-of-fact. Looking back later, we shall see some irony in the fact that the first words spoken by Brutus should warn Caesar of the ides of March. The date is significant for both men, but neither has any reason to suspect it yet.

24 Does this suggest that Caesar is not superstitious? Incidentally, we are not finished with this soothsayer.

S.D. *Sennet* a ceremonial sounding of trumpets, more elaborate than a flourish.

25 *the order of the course* how the running goes.

SCENE TWO

Flourish. Enter CAESAR; ANTONY, *stripped for racing*; CAL-
PHURNIA, PORTIA, DECIUS, CICERO, BRUTUS, CASSIUS, *and*
CASCA; *a great crowd following, among them a* Soothsayer;
after them MARULLUS *and* FLAVIUS

CAESAR: Calphurnia!

CASCA: Peace, ho! Caesar speaks.

CAESAR: Calphurnia!

CALPHURNIA: Here, my lord.

CAESAR: Stand you directly in Antonius' way,
  When he doth run his course. Antonius!

ANTONY: Caesar, my lord?   *5*

CAESAR: Forget not in your speed, Antonius,
  To touch Calphurnia; for our elders say,
  The barren, touched in this holy chase,
  Shake off their sterile curse

ANTONY: I shall remember.
  When Caesar says, 'Do this', it is performed.   *10*

CAESAR: Set on, and leave no ceremony out.   *Flourish*

SOOTHSAYER: Caesar!

CAESAR: Ha! Who calls?

CASCA: Bid every noise be still; peace yet again!

CAESAR: Who is it in the press that calls on me?   *15*
  I hear a tongue, shriller than all the music,
  Cry 'Caesar!' Speak; Caesar is turned to hear.

SOOTHSAYER: Beware the ides of March.

CAESAR: What man is that?

BRUTUS: A soothsayer bids you beware the ides of March.

CAESAR: Set him before me; let me see his face.   *20*

CASSIUS: Fellow, come from the throng; look upon Caesar.

CAESAR: What say'st thou to me now? Speak once again.

SOOTHSAYER: Beware the ides of March.

CAESAR: He is a dreamer; let us leave him. Pass.

          Sennet. Exeunt all except BRUTUS *and* CASSIUS

CASSIUS: Will you go see the order of the course?   *25*

28 *gamesome* interested in games. But the expression also suggests that Antony is frivolous. There is just the hint of a sneer—Brutus disapproves of frivolity.

32 Cassius is eyeing Brutus craftily as he speaks.

34 *as.* Relative pronoun; 'which' in modern usage.

35 A metaphor from horsemanship: you are handling me severely, like a stranger, not like a sympathetic rider on his own horse.

37 *veiled* put a veil over my face, so that I do not clearly show my feelings.

39 *Merely* entirely.

40 *passions of some difference* conflicting feelings.

41 ideas that belong to me alone; thoughts that I have no business to impose on anyone else.

42 *soil* blemish.

45 probe for any deeper meaning in my neglect.

47 The innocent Brutus hastens to assure Cassius of his unchanging friendship. Not yet realizing that Cassius has ulterior motives, he unwittingly gives him an opportunity of probing a little further.

48 *mistook.* This form of the past participle was right in Shakespeare's day.

49 because of which mistake I have kept hidden within myself. *whereof* refers to 'mistake' implied in *mistook.*

51 This kind of question appeals to Brutus; it seems to be leading to some interesting philosophical discussion.

54 exactly so.

55 it is widely regretted; many people regret.

57 *into your eye* into your range of vision.

58 *shadow* reflection.

60 *immortal* is sneeringly emphasized.

BRUTUS: Not I.

CASSIUS: I pray you, do.

BRUTUS: I am not gamesome; I do lack some part
  Of that quick spirit that is in Antony.
  Let me not hinder, Cassius, your desires;   30
  I'll leave you.

CASSIUS: Brutus, I do observe you now of late;
  I have not from your eyes that gentleness
  And show of love as I was wont to have.
  You bear too stubborn and too strange a hand   35
  Over your friend that loves you.

BRUTUS: Cassius,
  Be not deceived; if I have veiled my look,
  I turn the trouble of my countenance
  Merely upon myself. Vexed I am
  Of late with passions of some difference,   40
  Conceptions only proper to myself,
  Which give some soil, perhaps, to my behaviours;
  But let not therefore my good friends be grieved—
  Among which number, Cassius, be you one—
  Nor construe any further my neglect   45
  Than that poor Brutus, with himself at war,
  Forgets the shows of love to other men.

CASSIUS: Then, Brutus, I have much mistook your passion,
  By means whereof this breast of mine hath buried
  Thoughts of great value, worthy cogitations.   50
  Tell me, good Brutus, can you see your face?

BRUTUS: No, Cassius; for the eye sees not itself
  But by reflection, by some other things.

CASSIUS: 'T is just;
  And it is very much lamented, Brutus,   55
  That you have no such mirrors as will turn
  Your hidden worthiness into your eye,
  That you might see your shadow. I have heard,
  Where many of the best respect in Rome,
  Except immortal Caesar, speaking of Brutus,   60

62 have wished that noble Brutus could see himself as others see him.

63 Brutus with his keen mental powers instantly perceives the direction in which Cassius is moving, but characteristically will not be too hastily committed to anything.

66 *Therefore* may refer to Cassius' last words; he does not answer Brutus' question. Or, *therefore* means 'for that'; whether it is in you or not, you must decide when you have heard me out.

69 *Will modestly discover* will disclose moderately, without exaggeration.

71 *jealous on* suspicious of. *gentle* noble.

72 *a common laugher* one who jests with all and sundry; a frivolous light-minded person. *did use* was used, was accustomed.

73-74 *To stale . . . protester* to make stale my affection—destroy its fresh, attractive quality, therefore debase and cheapen it—by declaring it in trite, glib terms to anyone who asserts a liking for me on however brief acquaintance.

76 *after scandal* afterwards slander or decry them.

77-78 *That I profess . . . rout* that I profess friendship to all present in convivial company.

80 Cassius instantly seizes on the significant word.

82 Brutus cannot avoid declaring his view.

85 *the general good* the common weal, the good of the state.

87 *indifferently* with no different feelings. Therefore, I can look on honour and I can look on death with equal calmness.

88 *speed* prosper.

91 *outward favour* outward appearance. 'Favour' in Shakespeare frequently means face, aspect.

92 I am going to discourse on the present predicament of the honourable Roman.

94 Cassius' smouldering anger begins to take fire now. He drops some of the restraint he has with difficulty preserved so far, and the pace of the speech quickens.

95 *as lief not be* as soon not exist.

And groaning underneath this age's yoke,
Have wished that noble Brutus had his eyes.

BRUTUS: Into what dangers would you lead me, Cassius,
That you would have me seek into myself
For that which is not in me?   65

CASSIUS: Therefore, good Brutus, be prepared to hear;
And since you know you cannot see yourself
So well as by reflection, I, your glass,
Will modestly discover to yourself
That of yourself which you yet know not of.   70
And be not jealous on me, gentle Brutus;
Were I a common laugher, or did use
To stale with ordinary oaths my love
To every new protester; if you know
That I do fawn on men and hug them hard,   75
And after scandal them; or if you know
That I profess myself in banqueting
To all the rout, then hold me dangerous.
                                        Flourish and shout

BRUTUS: What means this shouting? I do fear, the people
Choose Caesar for their king.

CASSIUS: Ay, do you fear it?   80
Then must I think you would not have it so.

BRUTUS: I would not, Cassius; yet I love him well.
But wherefore do you hold me here so long?
What is it that you would impart to me?
If it be aught toward the general good,   85
Set honour in one eye, and death i' the other,
And I will look on both indifferently;
For let the gods so speed me as I love
The name of honour more than I fear death.

CASSIUS: I know that virtue to be in you, Brutus,   90
As well as I do know your outward favour.
Well, honour is the subject of my story.
I cannot tell what you and other men
Think of this life; but, for my single self,
I had as lief not be as live to be   95

100 The historical Caesar was a particularly strong swimmer. Is Shakespeare adapting history again? Does he want his Caesar to be less heroic than the real one? Or is Cassius not telling the truth?

101 Cf. 1.1.47.

105 *Accoutred* wearing all my equipment.

107 Caught up with his own story, Cassius achieves a fine vigorous picture here.

109 *hearts of controversy* hearts revelling in the struggle. There is a double meaning: the men are struggling against the water and against each other.

110 *arrive* reach. After a verb of motion modern usage often requires a preposition which Shakespeare could omit.

111–12 The actor makes a vivid contrast in tone—Caesar's piteous, weak cry, and then a sonorous reference to a noted hero of antiquity.

112 There was a tradition, supported by Vergil but not by Homer, that Aeneas, a refugee from Troy when it was burned by the Greeks, was the 'father and native god' of the Romans.

114 *Anchises* father of Aeneas.

115 Cassius repeats the pronoun 'I'—he already used it in line 112, emphasizing the similarity between himself and the legendary Aeneas; now he uses it again to have it alongside its verb.

118 The speech seems to finish here, and then another memory comes back to Cassius, and he forges ahead again.

121 *this god* spoken with heavy sarcasm.

122 It might be objected that it was the colour that fled from the lips. But the word *coward* suggested a soldier deserting the colours, and the confused expression not only manages to compress more than one idea into a concise form of words but also reflects vividly the speaker's intensity, which makes him pour out his ideas so fast that he can hardly find time to formulate them.

123 Not very different from the modern phrase, to bend one's gaze.

124 *his* its. 'His' was normal for neuter as well as masculine gender in Shakespeare's time. The modern word 'its' occurs only some half dozen times in his plays.

129 *temper* temperament, disposition.

131 Brutus puts out his hand to stop Cassius, and they listen for a moment to the confused noise of the crowd off stage. *bear the palm* carry off the reward for victory.

In awe of such a thing as I myself.
I was born free as Caesar; so were you;
We both have fed as well, and we can both
Endure the winter's cold as well as he.
For once, upon a raw and gusty day,   *100*
The troubled Tiber chafing with her shores,
Caesar said to me, 'Dar'st thou, Cassius, now
Leap in with me into this angry flood,
And swim to yonder point?' Upon the word,
Accoutred as I was, I plunged in   *dressed*   *105*
And bade him follow; so indeed he did.
The torrent roared, and we did buffet it
With lusty sinews, throwing it aside
And stemming it with hearts of controversy.
But ere we could arrive the point proposed,   *110*
Caesar cried, 'Help me, Cassius, or I sink!'
I, as Aeneas, our great ancestor,
Did from the flames of Troy upon his shoulder
The old Anchises bear, so from the waves of Tiber
Did I the tired Caesar. And this man   *115*
Is now become a god, and Cassius is
A wretched creature, and must bend his body   *bitterness*
If Caesar carelessly but nod on him.
He had a fever when he was in Spain,
And when the fit was on him, I did mark   *120*
How he did shake: 't is true, this god did shake;
His coward lips did from their colour fly,
And that same eye whose bend doth awe the world
Did lose his lustre; I did hear him groan;
Ay, and that tongue of his that bade the Romans   *125*
Mark him and write his speeches in their books,
Alas, it cried, 'Give me some drink, Titinius,'
As a sick girl. Ye gods! it doth amaze me
A man of such a feeble temper should
So get the start of the majestic world   *130*
And bear the palm alone.   *Shout. Flourish*

132 Brutus shows some agitation here.

134 This gives more fuel to Cassius, who rises to an even more picturesque comparison.

136 *Colossus.* One of the seven wonders of the ancient world, a huge statue over 100 feet high, erroneously believed to have stood astride the harbour of Rhodes.

Note the vigour of this passage, particularly the effectiveness of the word *peep*, with its miserable little sound.

140 Cassius has no patience with any form of predestination. He scorns the astrological view that a man's character and fate are determined by the relative positions of the stars and planets at the time of his birth.

143 why should that name be in men's mouths more than yours? But *sound* implies intonation—that the name is intoned, almost sung, given out ceremonially, with musical honour.

146 *conjure with them* use them to call up spirits, and you will find the name 'Caesar' has no more magical power than the name 'Brutus'.

152 *the great flood.* Shakespeare's audience would no doubt think at once of Noah. In fact the Romans had a similar legend, originally Greek, according to which Deucalion and Pyrrha preserved humanity.

153 *famed with* famous for.

156 A pun: 'Rome' in Shakespeare was pronounced 'room'. 'There is plenty of room in this city, for there is only one man in it; it is well named.'

159 Lucius Junius Brutus, from whom Brutus claimed descent, led the revolt against Tarquinius Superbus, the last king of Rome, in the sixth century B.C. The evil reputation of the Tarquins explains the horror of Brutus at the idea of Caesar assuming the title of king. *brooked* tolerated, suffered, permitted.

160-1 *The eternal devil* Satan. *to keep his state* to maintain his dignity; to lord it. The former Brutus would no more have accepted the rule of a king in Rome than he would have accepted the rule of Satan.

162 Cassius has ended a passionate tirade with a resounding climax. The answer of Brutus is slow, deliberate, quiet, every punctuation mark indicating a studied pause. But his voice rises, just a little, with firm emphasis at line 172. *am nothing jealous* have no doubt.

163 I can make a good shot at guessing what you would have me do.

166 if as a friend I may beg of you.

BRUTUS: Another general shout!
  I do believe that these applauses are
  For some new honours that are heaped on Caesar.
CASSIUS: Why, man, he doth bestride the narrow world   *135*
  Like a Colossus, and we petty men
  Walk under his huge legs, and peep about
  To find ourselves dishonourable graves.
  Men at some time are masters of their fates:
  The fault, dear Brutus, is not in our stars,   *140*
  But in ourselves, that we are underlings.
  Brutus and Caesar: what should be in that 'Caesar'?
  Why should that name be sounded more than yours?
  Write them together, yours is as fair a name;
  Sound them, it doth become the mouth as well;   *145*
  Weigh them, it is as heavy; conjure with 'em,
  'Brutus' will start a spirit as soon as 'Caesar'.
  Now, in the names of all the gods at once,
  Upon what meat doth this our Caesar feed,
  That he is grown so great? Age, thou art shamed!   *150*
  Rome, thou hast lost the breed of noble bloods!
  When went there by an age, since the great flood,
  But it was famed with more than with one man?
  When could they say, till now, that talked of Rome,
  That her wide walls encompassed but one man?   *155*
  Now is it Rome indeed, and room enough,
  When there is in it but one only man.
  O, you and I have heard our fathers say,
  There was a Brutus once that would have brooked
  The eternal devil to keep his state in Rome   *160*
  As easily as a king.
BRUTUS: That you do love me, I am nothing jealous;
  What you would work me to, I have some aim.
  How I have thought of this, and of these times,
  I shall recount hereafter. For this present,   *165*
  I would not, so with love I might entreat you,

167 Brutus will not allow himself to be carried away by emotion. He will take time to weigh all the considerations dispassionately and give a considered answer in due course.

171 *chew* ruminate.

172 *a villager* not a citizen. To a Roman, a citizen was a citizen of Rome—a highly prized title. A villager was a miserably inferior being—a barbarian.

173 *Than to repute himself* than claim the proud title of.

174 *as.* Rel. pron., 'which' in modern usage. Cf. line 34.

176 Despite his depreciatory words, Cassius has put everything he can into his great effort, and though he may seem to have struck little fire from Brutus in comparison with his own ardour, he knows well the man he is dealing with and is satisfied.

178 Brutus looks off stage in the direction from which the shouting has been heard, and both men move in that direction, towards the front of the stage.

180 A hint as to the character of Casca.

181 what has happened worthy of note.

S.D. As the following speech shows, all merriment is gone from the procession which now passes across the back of the stage. The people are uneasy and downcast. Caesar is glowering. Antony walks near him, silent and subdued. There is no conversation, and no trumpets sound. When Caesar is almost across the stage he stops (line 190); the rest stop too, and stand about in huddled groups, keeping well back from Caesar and Antony.

184 *a chidden train* a troop of subordinates who have been rebuked.

185 Though Cicero does not speak in this scene, this reference to him puts his name into our minds, and subconsciously this has an effect; when we hear of him again the name will be familiar, and we shall accept him as being of some importance.

186 *ferret.* Some commentators take this to mean red; but keen, piercing, flashing seems more appropriate—fierce.

188 *crossed in conference* opposed in debate.

195 An interesting remark. Is it not Brutus rather than Cassius who 'thinks too much'? A dictator can never like men who think too much; he requires unquestioning obedience, and people who insist on thinking for themselves cannot always agree with the decisions of authority. And certainly it is Cassius rather than Brutus who is dangerous to Caesar. Examine Caesar's remark very carefully.

197 *well given* well disposed. Antony enjoys life and does not look for trouble. Here he seems to underestimate Cassius.

199 Caesar claims to be immune from fear. Despite this arrogance, the following assessment of Cassius is shrewd.

[28]

Be any further moved. What you have said
I will consider; what you have to say
I will with patience hear, and find a time
Both meet to hear and answer such high things.   *170*
Till then, my noble friend, chew upon this:
Brutus had rather be a villager
Than to repute himself a son of Rome
Under these hard conditions as this time
Is like to lay upon us.   *175*

CASSIUS: I am glad that my weak words
  Have struck but thus much show of fire from Brutus.

BRUTUS: The games are done, and Caesar is returning.

CASSIUS: As they pass by, pluck Casca by the sleeve,
  And he will, after his sour fashion, tell you   *180*
  What hath proceeded worthy note to-day.

Re-enter CAESAR *and his train*

BRUTUS: I will do so. But, look you, Cassius,
  The angry spot doth glow on Caesar's brow,
  And all the rest look like a chidden train;
  Calphurnia's cheek is pale, and Cicero   *185*
  Looks with such ferret and such fiery eyes
  As we have seen him in the Capitol,
  Being crossed in conference by some Senators.

CASSIUS: Casca will tell us what the matter is.

CAESAR: Antonius!   *190*

ANTONY: Caesar?

CAESAR: Let me have men about me that are fat,
  Sleek-headed men, and such as sleep o' nights.
  Yond Cassius has a lean and hungry look;
  He thinks too much; such men are dangerous.   *195*

ANTONY: Fear him not, Caesar, he's not dangerous;
  He is a noble Roman, and well given.

CAESAR: Would he were fatter! But I fear him not.
  Yet if my name were liable to fear,
  I do not know the man I should avoid   *200*

[29]

203 *Quite through the deeds.* Cassius is not deceived by outward appearances: he can penetrate to the motives behind actions.

203-4 He has no interest in the pleasures of life. Shakespeare could hardly be expected to commend a man for his dislike of plays; as to his views on music, he tells us in 'The Merchant of Venice' that the man who has no music in himself is fit for treasons, and not to be trusted! Brutus, incidentally, likes music —cf. 4.3.255-56.

205 *sort* manner.

211 Caesar has almost revealed a human weakness in these fine lines, and now has to take command of himself again, reverting to the pose of line 199. The absurdity of the affectation is immediately exposed by the bathos of the next line—the god-like Caesar is deaf in one ear.

218 *sad* grave.

221 Casca at once justifies the description 'sour' of line 180. He speaks in prose; his account is deliberately derisive; verse would invest the story with too much dignity. This prose interlude affords a relief after the tension caused by the presence of Caesar.

229 *marry* an innocent exclamation, but originally an invocation of the Virgin Mary. *was't* was it; it was.

230 *honest* spoken ironically.

232 Cassius is interested in people. He opposes Caesar; he is ready to oppose the person who offered him the crown.

234 Brutus is placatory to Casca. He showed a similar spirit in his restrained answer at line 220.

So soon as that spare Cassius. He reads much,
He is a great observer, and he looks
Quite through the deeds of men. He loves no plays,
As thou dost, Antony; he hears no music.
Seldom he smiles, and smiles in such a sort   205
As if he mocked himself, and scorned his spirit
That could be moved to smile at anything.
Such men as he be never at heart's ease
Whiles they behold a greater than themselves,
And therefore are they very dangerous.   210
I rather tell thee what is to be feared
Than what I fear; for always I am Caesar.
Come on my right hand, for this ear is deaf,
And tell me truly what thou think'st of him.

Sennet. Exeunt CAESAR *and all his*
train, but CASCA

CASCA: You pulled me by the cloak. Would you speak with 215
me?

BRUTUS: Ay, Casca. Tell us what hath chanced to-day,
That Caesar looks so sad.

CASCA: Why, you were with him, were you not?

BRUTUS: I should not then ask Casca what had chanced.   220

CASCA: Why, there was a crown offered him; and being
offered him, he put it by with the back of his hand, thus;
and then the people fell a-shouting.

BRUTUS: What was the second noise for?

CASCA: Why, for that too.   225

CASSIUS: They shouted thrice; what was the last cry for?

CASCA: Why, for that too.

BRUTUS: Was the crown offered him thrice?

CASCA: Ay, marry, was 't, and he put it by thrice, every time
gentler than other, and at every putting-by mine honest 230
neighbours shouted.

CASSIUS: Who offered him the crown?

CASCA: Why, Antony.

BRUTUS: Tell us the manner of it, gentle Casca.

[31]

Opposite we see Cassius, Brutus, and Casca in Roman costume, as they are usually presented today. Casca is describing the crown that was offered to Caesar.

We seem to get a clear picture of Casca in this scene. He speaks prose, showing that the story he is telling has no emotional effect on him; he talks cynically of the whole business. This kind of account is highly amusing—it is always fun to speak of great men with contempt. Yet there are other glimpses of Casca, and remarks about him, which warn us to look deeper. He was 'quick mettle when he went to school', and he 'puts on this tardy form'. Besides, the man who ridicules Caesar in 1.2.221ff is the very man who bade the crowd be silent to hear Caesar at 1.2.1. In 1.3 he speaks verse, and seems much perturbed by the storm and the miracles he has seen.

The probable explanation is that in his youth Casca showed great promise, but has never fulfilled expectations, through some defect of character—lack of courage, perhaps, or concentration, or ambition. Such a man inwardly despises himself, and seeks to compensate for his inadequacy by acquiring a reputation for cynical comicality. No doubt when he cried 'Peace, ho! Caesar speaks' there was a sneer in his voice. He toadies to Caesar, and gives a comic account of the incident afterwards when Caesar is not there. His prose is part of his affectation, as Cassius realizes. In 1.3 the mask is off—he has been genuinely moved, and in verse shows evidence of his early promise. The scathing talk covers an underlying weakness which he secretly admits, and Casca finds himself compelled to do things which he deprecates even as he does them. Perhaps the commission to strike the first blow gives him for once a position of importance in which he can privately bask. But notice how soon he disappears from the play—we do not see him after 3.2. A man like Casca is essentially a second-rate sort of person, despite all the laughs he can raise.

A distinction has been made between Casca in prose and Casca in verse—Shakespeare's usual medium. Verse can compress more emotion and meaning into few words, it speeds the tempo and excites the hearer, and adds a musical effect to the literal meaning. And if it is spoken according to the punctuation it does not lapse into a mechanical sing-song, but sounds much more natural than its printed appearance may suggest.

235–49 Casca goes in for a certain amount of comic pantomime in his account. He gives the impression that he found the whole thing distasteful, but at least he gets some fun out of ridiculing it.

237 *not . . . neither* double negative, good English in Shakespeare's day.

239 *fain* gladly.

243 *still* always—common meaning in Shakespeare.

244 *chopt* chapped, cracked with exposure and hard work.

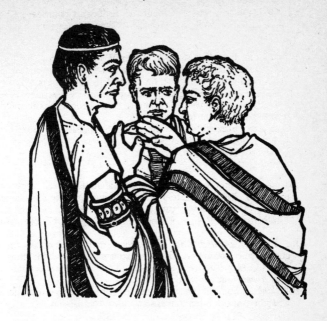

CASCA: I can as well be hanged as tell the manner of it; it was 235
mere foolery; I did not mark it. I saw Mark Antony offer
him a crown—yet 't was not a crown neither, 't was one of
these coronets—and, as I told you, he put it by once; but
for all that, to my thinking, he would fain have had it. Then
he offered it to him again; then he put it by again; but to 240
my thinking, he was very loath to lay his fingers off it. And
then he offered it the third time; he put it the third time by;
and still as he refused it, the rabblement hooted, and
clapped their chopt hands, and threw up their sweaty
night-caps, and uttered such a deal of stinking breath 245
because Caesar refused the crown, that it had almost
choked Caesar; for he swooned, and fell down at it. And for
mine own part, I durst not laugh, for fear of opening my
lips and receiving the bad air.

250 *soft* go easy; wait a moment. Again Cassius pounces on the opportunity to dwell on a physical weakness of Caesar.

253 *like* likely. *falling sickness* epilepsy. Brutus with characteristic reasonableness observes that Casca's story of Caesar falling down need give no surprise, for his epilepsy is well known.

255 Spoken with punning emphasis on *falling*. 'We are falling—Caesar is rising'. *honest* is a friendly term; Brutus, Cassius, and Casca are all decent fellows.

256 Is Casca puzzled, or does he choose to appear too matter-of-fact to follow such subtleties?

259 *use* are accustomed.

263 *me.* It is impossible to give an equivalent in modern language for this. It has a derogatory effect, and suggests the manner of speech. 'If you please' can be similarly spoken. *doublet* an Elizabethan, not Roman, garment, like a singlet, but thicker. *An* if.

264 *a man of any occupation* a practical man, hence a man with any capacity for action. Or, a working man, one of the crowd whom Caesar is addressing, instead of one of the aristocrats.

265 *at a word* at his word, literally.

268 *think it was his infirmity* put it down to his unfortunate disability, not to intention. An appeal to compassion.

276 Cicero in fact frequently did use Greek.

280-1 This is another affectation; Casca would know Greek perfectly well. But it was a good opportunity for a well-worn joke.

281-3 This comes as something of a shock. These two were so prominent in the opening scene that we thought they were going to figure a good deal in the play, and already they are obliterated. The episode shows that we are in a 'police state', where indiscretion is met with prompt and severe retribution.

282 *scarfs* streamers.

282-3 *put to silence* deprived of office, therefore rendered ineffectual.

286 *forth* out. I have promised to go out for supper.

[34]

CASSIUS: But soft, I pray you—what, did Caesar swoon? 250

CASCA: He fell down in the market-place, and foamed at mouth, and was speechless.

BRUTUS: 'Tis very like; he hath the falling sickness.

CASSIUS: No, Caesar hath it not; but you, and I,
And honest Casca, we have the falling sickness. 255

CASCA: I know not what you mean by that, but I am sure Caesar fell down. If the tag-rag people did not clap him and hiss him, according as he pleased and displeased them, as they use to do the players in the theatre, I am no true man.

BRUTUS: What said he when he came unto himself? 260

CASCA: Marry, before he fell down, when he perceived the common herd was glad he refused the crown, he plucked me ope his doublet and offered them his throat to cut. An I had been a man of any occupation, if I would not have taken him at a word, I would I might go to hell among the 265 rogues. And so he fell. When he came to himself again, he said, if he had done or said anything amiss, he desired their worships to think it was his infirmity. Three or four wenches, where I stood, cried, 'Alas, good soul!' and forgave him with all their hearts. But there's no heed to be 270 taken of them; if Caesar had stabbed their mothers, they would have done no less.

BRUTUS: And after that, he came thus sad away?

CASCA: Ay.

CASSIUS: Did Cicero say anything? 275

CASCA: Ay, he spoke Greek.

CASSIUS: To what effect?

CASCA: Nay, an I tell you that, I'll ne'er look you i' the face again. But those that understood him smiled at one another, and shook their heads; but for mine own part, it 280 was Greek to me. I could tell you more news too: Marullus and Flavius, for pulling scarfs off Caesar's images, are put to silence. Fare you well. There was more foolery yet, if I could remember it.

CASSIUS: Will you sup with me to-night, Casca? 285

CASCA: No, I am promised forth.

293 Again, as in 1.1.63, the double meaning of 'mettle' or 'metal' is brought into play by the use of another word, this time *blunt*.

296 no matter how much he pretends to be slow-witted.

297 *This rudeness is a sauce* this uncultured style adds a relish.

304 *the world* the general situation.

305 This passage is a soliloquy—that is, a speech made by a character when he is alone on the stage. The idea of having a person speak to nobody is not so absurd as it might seem. He is really thinking aloud—as some people do—and we can therefore be sure that we are hearing his true thoughts. When he is speaking to other people he may for various reasons not always tell the whole truth and nothing but the truth. The soliloquy may be an unsuitable device in realistic plays on the modern stage, where the actor is cut off from the audience by the barrier of the footlights and must project his voice to the back of the auditorium, but on the Elizabethan apron stage the actor would come to the front, and there, almost surrounded by the audience, he could speak musingly, and the situation would not seem unnatural. A similar effect is sometimes achieved in television plays, when the actor's voice is heard though his lips do not move—we understand that we are hearing his thoughts.

306-7 'As metal can be twisted into shapes it would not naturally take, so your honourable mettle can be pulled away from its natural course'.

307 *that it is* that to which it is.

309 who is so firm that he cannot be led astray?

310 *bear me hard* bear ill will towards me.

311 Cassius frankly admits that he and Caesar are enemies, Brutus and Caesar are friends. In Brutus' place, therefore, he would not allow himself to be turned against Caesar. But this reflection does not deter him from his seduction of Brutus. The passage, however, is ambiguous. Work out other possible interpretations.

312 *humour* manipulate; work round to his way of thinking.

313 *hands* styles of handwriting.

317 *glanced* hinted.

318 *seat him sure* seat himself firmly.

319 Either, we will shake him or take the consequences of being foiled, or, the future is sure to be worse than the present if Caesar is allowed to remain in power.

The rhyming couplet to end the scene is common—it is an easily memorised cue for the actors who are to start the next scene. Here it also has a decisive quality which perfectly suits the grim determination of Cassius, and gives the scene a strong finish.

CASSIUS: Will you dine with me to-morrow?

CASCA: Ay, if I be alive, and your mind hold, and your
    dinner worth the eating.

CASSIUS: Good; I will expect you.   290

CASCA: Do so. Farewell, both.   *Exit*

BRUTUS: What a blunt fellow is this grown to be!
    He was quick mettle when he went to school.

CASSIUS: So is he now in execution
    Of any bold or noble enterprise,   295
    However he puts on this tardy form.
    This rudeness is a sauce to his good wit,
    Which gives men stomach to digest his words
    With better appetite.

BRUTUS: And so it is. For this time I will leave you.   300
    To-morrow, if you please to speak with me,
    I will come home to you; or, if you will,
    Come home to me, and I will wait for you.

CASSIUS: I will do so. Till then, think of the world.

                          Exit BRUTUS

    Well, Brutus, thou art noble; yet I see   305
    Thy honourable metal may be wrought
    From that it is disposed. Therefore 'tis meet
    That noble minds keep ever with their likes;
    For who so firm that cannot be seduced?
    Caesar doth bear me hard; but he loves Brutus: 310
    If I were Brutus now and he were Cassius,
    He should not humour me. I will this night,
    In several hands, in at his windows throw,
    As if they came from several citizens,
    Writings, all tending to the great opinion   315
    That Rome holds of his name; wherein obscurely
    Caesar's ambition shall be glanced at.
    And after this let Caesar seat him sure,
    For we will shake him, or worse days endure.   *Exit*

In Scene Two we met a number of important people, but it was possible to gain some quite distinct impressions of them. The first speaker was Caesar. He was not long on the stage, but while there he dominated the proceedings. He called for Calphurnia and Antony by name. Calphurnia spoke only three words. Do you remember what they were? What do you make of the relationship between Caesar and his wife? Antony said little more. What is his attitude to Caesar? Casca, Brutus, and Cassius had a few words each—just enough to draw our attention to them. There was a long and significant conversation between Brutus and Cassius. Then Casca revealed some of his complex character in prose and explained the important things that had been happening off stage. The crowd played their part in adding atmosphere too, even when we only heard them as 'noises off'. Finally, we had the ominous soliloquy of Cassius—evidently we are going to have plenty of action soon.

A street

3 *sway* sovereignty. The established order of the great globe itself is quaking—how then can Cicero remain unmoved? This agitated Casca is strangely different from the dry cynic of the last scene. He is speaking in verse now—this in itself proves that he is emotionally stirred. Indeed, he appears thoroughly scared.

6 *rived* cleft.

12 *saucy* presumptuous.

14 This line is ambiguous; *more* could go with *anything* or with *wonderful*. Both meanings show that Cicero is not greatly impressed. No doubt Shakespeare, who was present at the rehearsals of his plays and perhaps actually produced them, would tell the original actor how to speak the line.

18 *Not sensible of fire* not feeling heat.

20 *Against* close by.

21 *glazed* gazed with a glassy look.

22 *annoying* molesting.

23 *Upon a heap* packed close together.

26 *the bird of night* the owl; an evil omen when it appeared by day.

28 *prodigies* extraordinary, ominous things.

29 *conjointly meet* happen all at once.

30 'Such and such are the reasons for these things; they can all be explained according to the normal laws of nature.'

31 *portentous* ominous; full of grim prediction.

32 *climate* clime; region.

SCENE THREE

Thunder and lightning. Enter, from opposite sides, CASCA, *with his sword drawn, and* CICERO

CICERO: Good even, Casca. Brought you Caesar home?
  Why are you breathless? and why stare you so?
CASCA: Are not you moved, when all the sway of earth
  Shakes like a thing unfirm? O Cicero,
  I have seen tempests, when the scolding winds   *5*
  Have rived the knotty oaks; and I have seen
  The ambitious ocean swell and rage and foam,
  To be exalted with the threatening clouds;
  But never till to-night, never till now,
  Did I go through a tempest dropping fire.   *10*
  Either there is a civil strife in heaven,
  Or else the world, too saucy with the gods,
  Incenses them to send destruction.
CICERO: Why, saw you anything more wonderful?
CASCA: A common slave—you know him well by sight—   *15*
  Held up his left hand, which did flame and burn
  Like twenty torches joined; and yet his hand,
  Not sensible of fire, remained unscorched.
  Besides—I have not since put up my sword—
  Against the Capitol I met a lion,   *20*
  Who glazed upon me, and went surly by,
  Without annoying me. And there were drawn
  Upon a heap a hundred ghastly women,
  Transformed with their fear, who swore they saw
  Men, all in fire, walk up and down the streets.   *25*
  And yesterday the bird of night did sit
  Even at noon-day, upon the market-place,
  Hooting and shrieking. When these prodigies
  Do so conjointly meet, let not men say,
  'These are their reasons; they are natural';   *30*
  For I believe they are portentous things
  Unto the climate that they point upon.

33 *strange-disposed* strangely ordered.

34–5 'Men may interpret things according to their own ideas, reading in meanings not really inherent in the things themselves.' A sane view of a philosopher who has cultivated an unemotional, detached approach.

39 *sky* atmosphere.

40 is not fit to walk in.

41 Here we have scene-painting in the dialogue. Shakespeare's theatre was open to the sky, and plays were performed in daylight. The audience were adept at picking up hints from the dialogue; this line would tell them that the action is supposed to take place in darkness. Did you notice that the first words of the scene told us the time of day? Watch for similar instances later.

42 *what night* what a night.

43–5 Cassius accepts the implication that the thunderstorm demonstrates the anger of the gods against erring mankind, but having a clear conscience he has nothing to fear. In contrast to Casca, Cassius seems to see the storm as a challenge and is stimulated, as adventurous spirits see the approach of danger with relish.

48 *unbraced* unbuttoned. Again the word seems more appropriate to Elizabethan than to Roman costume, but it could be a general term for loosened clothing.

49 *thunder-stone* thunderbolt.

50 *cross* forked.

51–2 In his elation Cassius dares the heavens, triumphantly confident that their threats are not directed at him.

57 *dull* slow to understand. This is not a judgement of Casca's general nature (cf. 1.2.293–96), but applies only to this particular episode as Cassius is going to present it.

58 *want* lack.

59 *Or else you use not* or else you do not make use of your lively talents.

60 *cast yourself in wonder* put yourself into a state of amazement. To cast is to pour molten metal into a mould.

63–4 Verbs must be supplied: why (there are) all these fires, why (there are) all these gliding ghosts; why birds and beasts (depart) from quality and kind, i.e., act unlike themselves.

64 *quality and kind* character and nature.

CICERO: Indeed, it is a strange-disposed time;
   But men may construe things after their fashion,
   Clean from the purpose of the things themselves.   *35*
   Comes Caesar to the Capitol to-morrow?
CASCA: He doth; for he did bid Antonius
   Send word to you he would be there to-morrow.
CICERO: Good night then, Casca; this disturbed sky
   Is not to walk in.
CASCA: Farewell, Cicero.   *Exit* CICERO *40*

Enter CASSIUS

CASSIUS: Who's there?
CASCA: A Roman.
CASSIUS: Casca, by your voice.
CASCA: Your ear is good. Cassius, what night is this!
CASSIUS: A very pleasing night to honest men.
CASCA: Who ever knew the heavens menace so?
CASSIUS: Those that have known the earth so full of faults.   *45*
   For my part, I have walked about the streets,
   Submitting me unto the perilous night,
   And, thus unbraced, Casca, as you see,
   Have bared my bosom to the thunder-stone;
   And when the cross blue lightning seemed to open   *50*
   The breast of heaven, I did present myself
   Even in the aim and very flash of it.
CASCA: But wherefore did you so much tempt the heavens?
   It is the part of men to fear and tremble
   When the most mighty gods by token send   *55*
   Such dreadful heralds to astonish us.
CASSIUS: You are dull, Casca, and those sparks of life
   That should be in a Roman you do want,
   Or else you use not. You look pale, and gaze,
   And put on fear, and cast yourself in wonder,   *60*
   To see the strange impatience of the heavens;
   But if you would consider the true cause
   Why all these fires, why all these gliding ghosts,
   Why birds and beasts from quality and kind,

65 Old men (meaning dotards), fools, and children are all unfit to calculate, i.e., interpret astrological signs, therefore they too are acting unlike themselves.

66 *ordinance*   what is ordained; proper behaviour.

67 *preformed faculties*   the powers with which they were born.

68 *monstrous*   unnatural, abnormal.

71 *Unto some monstrous state*   of some threatened unnatural state of affairs.

75 The lion seen by Casca (line 20), though Cassius was not present when Casca told Cicero about it; normally there was no lion in the Capitol. Perhaps Shakespeare was thinking of the lions in the Tower of London, a popular sight in his day.

77 *prodigious*   of more than human significance.

78 *eruptions*   outbreaks.

57-78 How expertly Cassius takes his opportunity! He makes Casca ashamed of himself by describing him as a poor-spirited creature who has wilted before the onslaught of the storm and the miraculous events. Then he describes these events, not belittling them, but on the contrary magnifying them in the mounting series of 'why' clauses until he comes to a climax in the ominous short line 71. By now Casca is even more frightened; he sorely needs some explanation of all this, which now seems even worse than he had realised. Cassius drops his voice to a menacing, crafty low tone as he reveals the meaning of it all, and Casca gratefully seizes the disclosure, in an outburst of relief at finding that it is not at him that the supernatural wrath is aimed.

79 Cassius, more wily, does not mention names. Casca, more ingenuous, does. It is dangerous in a dictatorship to name the dictator unless in complimentary terms.

81 *thews*   sinews, muscles.

84 *Our yoke and sufferance*   our servitude and uncomplaining endurance.

89 Cassius will commit suicide rather than submit to what he considers disgrace. The willingness to do this was highly characteristic of the Romans; the idea occurs several times in this play, and in *Macbeth* when the hero thinks of suicide he calls it playing 'the Roman fool'.

89-100 When working on Brutus in the previous scene Cassius put forth his finest rhetoric. Now he is working on Casca, and he uses the same method. Note the word-play in lines 90-2, the emphasis gained by the balancing of lines 91 and 92, and the mounting expressions of lines 93-4.

91 *Therein*   in the power to take one's own life.

95 *Can be retentive to*   can hold in.

96 *these worldly bars*   the bars of the imprisoning world.

[42]

Why old men, fools, and children calculate, 65
Why all these things change from their ordinance
Their natures, and preformed faculties,
To monstrous quality, why, you shall find
That heaven hath infused them with these spirits
To make them instruments of fear and warning 70
Unto some monstrous state.
Now could I, Casca, name to thee a man
Most like this dreadful night
That thunders, lightens, opens graves, and roars
As doth the lion in the Capitol; 75
A man no mightier than thyself or me
In personal action, yet prodigious grown,
And fearful, as these strange eruptions are.

CASCA: 'T is Caesar that you mean; is it not, Cassius?

CASSIUS: Let it be who it is; for Romans now 80
Have thews and limbs like to their ancestors;
But, woe the while! our fathers' minds are dead,
And we are governed with our mothers' spirits;
Our yoke and sufferance show us womanish.

CASCA: Indeed, they say the Senators to-morrow 85
Mean to establish Caesar as a king;
And he shall wear his crown by sea and land,
In every place, save here in Italy.

CASSIUS: I know where I will wear this dagger, then;
Cassius from bondage will deliver Cassius. 90
Therein, ye gods, you make the weak most strong;
Therein, ye gods, you tyrants do defeat.
Nor stony tower, nor walls of beaten brass,
Nor airless dungeon, nor strong links of iron,
Can be retentive to the strength of spirit; 95
But life, being weary of these worldly bars,
Never lacks power to dismiss itself.

98 *know all the world* let all the world know.

102 *cancel* annul. This is a legal term. We speak of annulling a bond, a legal document, and Casca contrives a neat suggestion of a pun, having just used the word 'bond' in *bondman*, a prisoner in chains.

106 *hinds* female deer; timid, subservient animals. Again there is a double meaning: a hind was also a servant or a boor. The reference to Caesar as a lion is particularly apt, the lion being the 'king of beasts'.

108-9 *trash . . . rubbish . . . offal.* All of these are appropriate in the idea of making a fire. Trash was useless twigs, etc. from felled trees, offal (derived from 'off fall') could mean chips of wood.

111 *vile* mean, worthless.

104-11 Cassius again builds up his argument with beautiful artistry. Notice the balanced comparisons—wolf and sheep, lion and hinds, mighty fire and weak straws—all richly imaginative ideas. Again he makes a telling climax—'So vile a thing as Caesar'—followed by a dramatic halt and change of tone.

111-15 Cassius has indeed been speaking with profound feeling, particularly from line 89. Has he in fact been carried further than he had intended? If Casca is loyal to Caesar, Cassius has placed himself in danger of an accusation of treason. Or, has his intellect kept his emotion in control all the time? If it has, these lines are designed to force a declaration from Casca.

115 *indifferent* of no importance.

117 *fleering* giggling. *Hold* enough! *my hand* here is my hand.

118 *Be factious* form a militant group.

120 *who.* Rel. pron. Antecedent 'he' to be supplied. They shake hands, and at the end of the line Cassius pauses, looking intently into Casca's eyes. This is another moment of success—another ally is gained. At line 121 he changes to a more confidential tone.

123 *undergo* undertake.

125 *by this* by this time.

126 *Pompey's porch* the porchway of Pompey's theatre.

128 *complexion* condition. *element.* Shakespeare sometimes uses this term in its medieval sense of 'primary substance'—earth, air, fire, water—but also as here in the sense of atmosphere or sky.

129 *favour* appearance. Cf. 1.2.91.

131 *Stand close* keep under cover. In the Elizabethan theatre they would retreat into the 'inner stage'.

    If I know this, know all the world besides,
    That part of tyranny that I do bear
    I can shake off at pleasure.   *More thunder*
CASCA: So can I;   *100*
    So every bondman in his own hand bears
    The power to cancel his captivity.
CASSIUS: And why should Caesar be a tyrant then?
    Poor man! I know he would not be a wolf,
    But that he sees the Romans are but sheep;   *105*
    He were no lion, were not Romans hinds.
    Those that with haste will make a mighty fire
    Begin it with weak straws. What trash is Rome,
    What rubbish, and what offal, when it serves
    For the base matter to illuminate   *110*
    So vile a thing as Caesar! But, O grief,
    Where hast thou led me? I perhaps speak this
    Before a willing bondman; then I know
    My answer must be made. But I am armed,
    And dangers are to me indifferent.   *115*
CASCA: You speak to Casca, and to such a man
    That is no fleering tell-tale. Hold, my hand.
    Be factious for redress of all these griefs,
    And I will set this foot of mine as far
    As who goes farthest.
CASSIUS: There's a bargain made.   *120*
    Now know you, Casca, I have moved already
    Some certain of the noblest-minded Romans
    To undergo with me an enterprise
    Of honourable-dangerous consequence;
    And I do know, by this they stay for me   *125*
    In Pompey's porch; for now, this fearful night,
    There is no stir or walking in the streets;
    And the complexion of the element
    In favour's like the work we have in hand,
    Most bloody, fiery, and most terrible.   *130*
CASCA: Stand close awhile, for here comes one in haste.

132 Note how this line and the end of line 41 bear out 1.2.202.

135-6 *incorporate To our attempts* who has joined forces with us; a collaborator.

137 *I am glad on't* I am glad that Casca has joined us.

137-41 Cinna is finding some difficulty in concentrating. He has come to find Cassius, but does not say why; he omits to answer Cassius' question, and it has to be repeated. He wants to talk about the strange sights, but Cassius has other things to deal with, and cuts him short. Cinna does deliver his message now, but only with half his mind, and off he shoots at once to another subject.

142 *Be you content* set your mind at rest.

143 see that you put it in the magistrate's chair.

144 *Brutus may but find it* only Brutus may find it, or, Brutus may find it by chance.

146 *old Brutus.* See 1.2.159.

150 *hie* hurry.

151 It is to be hoped that Cinna will remember his instructions!

156 *yields him ours* surrenders himself to us.

157 Casca's tribute to Brutus reinforces the thought of Cinna at lines 140-1.

159 *alchemy* the medieval science devoted to the problem of turning base metals into gold.

162 *conceited* conceived; understood.

At the end of the First Act the exposition should be complete—that is, we should know what the play is about, and we should have some idea of the main characters. In this scene one new character is introduced—Cicero. Shakespeare gives no indication as to the ages of most of the characters in this play, and history is not much guide, since Shakespeare as we have seen accepts history as far as he likes and no further. But later he does make a point of Cicero's 'silver hairs'; let us then imagine him as in fact he was at this time—a man of about sixty. We heard in Scene Two that he could on occasion display anger, but here he is perfectly controlled and placid, unlike Casca, amid the tumult of the ominous storm. The conspiracy gains another recruit in Casca, and at the close of the scene we feel confident that Brutus will soon be in it too. It is clear that Cinna and Casca are as anxious as Cassius to secure him. Now we know our men, and we know what is in hand. The next question is, will Brutus join the company?

CASSIUS: 'Tis Cinna, I do know him by his gait;
  He is a friend.

Enter CINNA

             Cinna, where haste you so?
CINNA: To find out you. Who's that? Metellus Cimber?
CASSIUS: No, it is Casca; one incorporate   *135*
  To our attempts. Am I not stayed for, Cinna?
CINNA: I am glad on't. What a fearful night is this!
  There's two or three of us have seen strange sights.
CASSIUS: Am I not stayed for? Tell me.
CINNA: Yes, you are. O Cassius, if you could   *140*
  But win the noble Brutus to our party—
CASSIUS: Be you content. Good Cinna, take this paper,
  And look you lay it in the praetor's chair,
  Where Brutus may but find it; and throw this
  In at his window; set this up with wax   *145*
  Upon old Brutus' statue. All this done,
  Repair to Pompey's porch, where you shall find us.
  Is Decius Brutus and Trebonius there?
CINNA: All but Metellus Cimber, and he's gone
  To seek you at your house. Well, I will hie,   *150*
  And so bestow these papers as you bade me.
CASSIUS: That done, repair to Pompey's theatre.   *Exit* CINNA
  Come, Casca, you and I will yet ere day
  See Brutus at his house. Three parts of him
  Is ours already, and the man entire   *155*
  Upon the next encounter yields him ours.
CASCA: O, he sits high in all the people's hearts;
  And that which would appear offence in us,
  His countenance, like richest alchemy,
  Will change to virtue and to worthiness.   *160*
CASSIUS: Him and his worth and our great need of him
  You have right well conceited. Let us go,
  For it is after midnight; and ere day
  We will awake him and be sure of him.   *Exeunt*

Rome. Brutus' orchard

There is no thunder now, but in a modern production we are reminded of the storm by an occasional flash of lightning.

1 *What.* This impatient exclamation has no literal meaning.

5 *When.* This too is an impatient exclamation: When are you going to answer?

7 *taper* candle.

10 Study this soliloquy very carefully. Critics vary sharply in their views: some accuse Brutus of confusion and self-deception, others find it admirable in its clarity and logic. Analyse it step by step and form your own conclusion.

11 *spurn* kick. The contrast is between the personal and the general. I have no personal reason to rebel against him, but it may be desirable for the general good.

12 *general* general public; the common weal. *would be* would willingly be.

15 *that craves* the adder calls for. *that—* suppose that is done.

14–17 A good metaphor. The bright day brings out the adder: the most promising circumstances produce their own particular hazards. So Caesar's rising fortunes may reveal dangerous qualities in him not yet evident. The bright day is the prosperous, splendid day; if Caesar is crowned he will be in a blaze of prosperity and splendour. That is when the insidious deadly capacity of the man can be expected to creep out.

19 *Remorse* compassion; not repentance. It is common for great men to misuse their position by failing to show consideration for those under them. Brutus the philosopher states a general principle first and then applies it to the particular case. Tyrants commonly become oppressors; if Caesar gains such power he may become oppressive.

20 *affections* feelings generally. I have never known him to allow his heart (his desires) to overrule his head (his reason). Note how scrupulous Brutus is. He is making every effort to weigh the situation accurately. So far, Caesar has shown no sign of oppressiveness.

21 *common proof* a thing regularly proved by experience.

22 The ambitious young man cultivates a reputation for humility as a means of advancement. Is Caesar feigning humility then as a means to an end?

24 *upmost round* topmost rung.

ACT TWO

SCENE ONE

Enter BRUTUS

BRUTUS: What, Lucius, ho!
  I cannot by the progress of the stars
  Give guess how near to day.—Lucius, I say!
  I would it were my fault to sleep so soundly.—
  When, Lucius, when? Awake, I say! What, Lucius!   *5*

Enter LUCIUS

LUCIUS: Called you, my lord?
BRUTUS: Get me a taper in my study, Lucius;
  When it is lighted, come and call me here.
LUCIUS: I will, my lord.   *Exit*
BRUTUS: It must be by his death; and for my part,   *10*
  I know no personal cause to spurn at him,
  But for the general. He would be crowned:
  How that might change his nature, there's the question.
  It is the bright day that brings forth the adder,
  And that craves wary walking. Crown him—that—   *15*
  And then, I grant, we put a sting in him
  That at his will he may do danger with.
  The abuse of greatness is when it disjoins
  Remorse from power; and, to speak truth of Caesar,
  I have not known when his affections swayed   *20*
  More than his reason. But 't is a common proof
  That lowliness is young ambition's ladder,
  Whereto the climber-upward turns his face;
  But when he once attains the upmost round,
  He then unto the ladder turns his back,   *25*

[49]

25–27 We picture the man stepping off the ladder on to some eminence, and forgetting all about the means whereby he has climbed—i.e., his humility.

26 *base degrees* low steps.

28 *prevent* anticipate, and so forestall. *quarrel* case for complaint. The case against Caesar as he actually is will not be convincing.

29 *bear no colour* carry no justification.

30 *Fashion it* formulate it.

33 *as his kind* as serpents do; according to the natural law of the breed. An adder is a kind of serpent; the argument has returned to the idea of line 14, and ends with a restatement of the first words, now reinforced by all this reasoning.

35 *closet* private room; study.

40 *the ides of March.* We heard these words before. When?

44 *exhalations* meteors. To exhale is to breathe out; but it formerly also meant to draw out. The sun was believed to draw vapours from the earth and to convert them somehow into meteors.

44–5 In the opening lines of the scene we learned that the action is taking place in darkness. These two lines are therefore necessary to explain how Brutus can read the letter he is now given. Is this a neat or a clumsy contrivance?

46 Cf. 1.2.51–70.

47 *etcetera.* This presents a difficulty. It could be actually written in the letter, but if so it seems unnecessarily vague. Perhaps the actor should stop reading at this point with an expression like 'and so on', suggesting that what follows is all the usual stuff he has heard before.

49–50 It would seem that Brutus unquestioningly accepts these letters as coming from different Romans. Is this evidence of a noble nature or of foolish simplicity?

51 *piece it out* fill in the *etcetera*.

52 *under one man's awe* in awe of one man.

56 Brutus could clasp his hands as though in an attitude of prayer.

56–8 Brutus is very near decision. He is prepared to go all the way if he can feel confident that his action will bring a remedy for the evils he foresees.

Looks in the clouds, scorning the base degrees
By which he did ascend. So Caesar may.
Then, lest he may, prevent. And, since the quarrel
Will bear no colour for the thing he is,
Fashion it thus: that what he is, augmented,   *30*
Would run to these and these extremities;
And therefore think him as a serpent's egg,
Which, hatched, would, as his kind, grow mischievous,
And kill him in the shell.

Re-enter LUCIUS

LUCIUS: The taper burneth in your closet, sir.   *35*
Searching the window for a flint, I found
This paper, thus sealed up; and I am sure
It did not lie there when I went to bed.
Gives him a letter

BRUTUS: Get you to bed again; it is not day.
Is not to-morrow, boy, the ides of March?   *40*
LUCIUS: I know not, sir.
BRUTUS: Look in the calendar, and bring me word.
LUCIUS: I will, sir.   *Exit*
BRUTUS: The exhalations whizzing in the air
Give so much light that I may read by them.   *45*
Opens the letter and reads
'Brutus, thou sleep'st; awake, and see thyself.
Shall Rome, etcetera. Speak, strike, redress!'
'Brutus, thou sleep'st; awake!'
Such instigations have been often dropped
Where I have took them up.   *50*
'Shall Rome, etcetera.' Thus must I piece it out:
Shall Rome stand under one man's awe? What, Rome?
My ancestors did from the streets of Rome
The Tarquin drive, when he was called a king.
'Speak, strike, redress!' Am I entreated   *55*
To speak and strike? O Rome, I make thee promise:
If the redress will follow, thou receivest
Thy full petition at the hand of Brutus!

[51]

59 *S.D. within*   off stage.

64 *the first motion*   the first stirrings of the idea in the mind. *interim*   interval, time between.

65 *phantasma*   nightmare; no different from *a hideous dream*.

66 *genius*   guardian angel, or essential nature. *mortal instruments* physical powers; mortal as opposed to the immortal genius.

67 *in council*   in debate, therefore not in harmony. *state*.   Not condition, but a political unit, explained by the following phrase *little kingdom*. The analogy between the individual and the state has been used by many writers, and especially suits this political play.

69 *The nature of an insurrection*   an experience that can be compared to a rebellion. Remember all the political plotting of Elizabeth's reign; to loyal subjects (like Shakespeare) the idea of rebellion would be not only topical but frightening.

70 *brother*   brother-in-law. Shakespeare uses the word in this sense elsewhere. Cassius had married Brutus' sister.

72 *moe*   more.

73 *hats*.   This sounds like an anachronism, but the Romans did wear headgear, and 'hat' could no doubt be used as the general term, though 'cap' would perhaps seem more appropriate to us. It is not necessary to imagine the conspirators looking like Guy Fawkes and company.

75 *That*   so that. *discover*   identify, pierce the disguise.

77 *faction*   the conspirators. Cf. 1.3.118.

79 *evils are most free*   evil things are most at liberty.

81 *monstrous*   unnatural, therefore horrible.

83 *path*   go ahead. The word is uncommon but not unknown as a verb. *thy native semblance on*   wearing your own appearance; showing yourself as you really are.

84 *Erebus*   a murky region of the underworld through which the spirits of the dead had to pass.

85 *prevention*   being forestalled and thwarted.

Re-enter LUCIUS

LUCIUS: Sir, March is wasted fourteen days.

Knocking within

BRUTUS: 'T is good. Go to the gate; somebody knocks.   60

Exit LUCIUS

Since Cassius first did whet me against Caesar
I have not slept.
Between the acting of a dreadful thing
And the first motion, all the interim is
Like a phantasma, or a hideous dream.   65
The genius and the mortal instruments
Are then in council; and the state of man,
Like to a little kingdom, suffers then
The nature of an insurrection.

Re-enter LUCIUS

LUCIUS: Sir, 't is your brother Cassius at the door,   70
Who doth desire to see you.

BRUTUS: Is he alone?

LUCIUS: No, sir, there are moe with him.

BRUTUS: Do you know them?

LUCIUS: No, sir; their hats are plucked about their ears,
And half their faces buried in their cloaks,
That by no means I may discover them   75
By any mark of favour.

BRUTUS: Let 'em enter.   *Exit* LUCIUS

They are the faction. O conspiracy,
Shamest thou to show thy dangerous brow by night,
When evils are most free? O, then by day
Where wilt thou find a cavern dark enough   80
To mask thy monstrous visage? Seek none, **conspiracy**;
Hide it in smiles and affability;
For if thou path, thy native semblance on,
Not Erebus itself were dim enough
To hide thee from prevention.   85

[53]

86 *are too bold upon your rest*   are taking a liberty by intruding upon your rest.

89 This question shows that the men's faces are still hidden in their cloaks. Cassius will come in first and go quickly to Brutus, the others following more slowly while Cassius is speaking. The last of them will scarcely be in when Brutus speaks. They will uncover their faces before being presented to Brutus.

90 *no man here*   there is no man here.

98 *watchful cares*   wakeful cares; cares that keep one awake.

101–11 A masterly little passage. The two leaders are conferring privately; the others must talk, because silence would be embarrassing—they might appear to be eavesdropping, but, more important, in their present state of tension they cannot bear to be left alone with their thoughts, which inevitably return to the insistent subject of murder. What then are they to talk about? Casting around desperately for some excuse for a remark, Decius can do no better than ask an idle question. Immediately the topic is seized upon and debated; despite its intrinsic triviality it is of supreme importance in providing the necessary diversion.

102 The blunt Casca.

104 *fret.*   An architectural term accurately used: to decorate a ceiling with a pattern in fine lines.

107 *growing on*   coming by degrees towards.

108 *Weighing*   taking into consideration.

114 Note this difference of opinion. In itself it does not seem very significant, but it is the first of a number of differences which in total are of decisive importance. *If not . . .* Brutus recasts this sentence as he is speaking; it is not grammatical. *the face of men* the sad faces men are wearing.

115 *sufferance*   suffering. *the time's abuse*   the wrongs prevalent at this time.

116 *betimes*   in good time.

Enter the conspirators, CASSIUS, CASCA, DECIUS, CINNA,
METELLUS CIMBER, *and* TREBONIUS

CASSIUS: I think we are too bold upon your rest.
    Good morrow, Brutus. Do we trouble you?

BRUTUS: I have been up this hour, awake all night.
    Know I these men that come along with you?

CASSIUS: Yes, every man of them, and no man here   *90*
    But honours you; and every one doth wish
    You had but that opinion of yourself
    Which every noble Roman bears of you.
    This is Trebonius.

BRUTUS: He is welcome hither.

CASSIUS: This, Decius Brutus.

BRUTUS: He is welcome too.   *95*

CASSIUS: This, Casca; this, Cinna; and this, Metellus Cimber.

BRUTUS: They are all welcome.
    What watchful cares do interpose themselves
    Betwixt your eyes and night?

CASSIUS: Shall I entreat a word?   *100*

                    BRUTUS and CASSIUS move aside

DECIUS: Here lies the east; doth not the day break here?

CASCA: No.

CINNA: O, pardon, sir, it doth; and yon grey lines
    That fret the clouds are messengers of day.

CASCA: You shall confess that you are both deceived.   *105*
    Here, as I point my sword, the sun arises,
    Which is a great way growing on the south,
    Weighing the youthful season of the year.
    Some two months hence, up higher toward the north
    He first presents his fire; and the high east   *110*
    Stands, as the Capitol, directly here.

BRUTUS: Give me your hands all over, one by one.

CASSIUS: And let us swear our resolution.

BRUTUS: No, not an oath. If not the face of men,
    The sufferance of our souls, the time's abuse,—   *115*
    If these be motives weak, break off betimes,
    And every man hence to his idle bed.

118 *high-sighted* looking from on high, like a falcon. *range* roam at large.

119 *by lottery* by chance. The tyrant will destroy men according to his own whim, whether they have deserved their fate or not. *these* as in line 116.

123 Two constructions condensed: 'Do we need any spur?' and 'What spur do we need?'

124 *What other bond* what other bond do we need.

125 *Than secret Romans* than that we are secret Romans. *secret* able to keep a secret; trustworthy.

126 *palter* equivocate. They will stand firmly by their word, and not pretend that they meant something else.

127 than an undertaking between honest people.

129 let priests and cowards and treacherous men swear.

130 *carrions* corpses; decrepit old men as near death as makes no difference.

131 *That* 'as' in modern usage.

133 *even* smooth, therefore unblemished; pure.

134 *insuppressive* insuppressible. The -ive suffix for the modern -ible is fairly common in Shakespeare and Milton.

135 *To think* by thinking. *or . . . or* either . . . or.

138 individually reveals him to be no true son of Rome.

140 If you were one of the conspirators, what would you make of this? Brutus seems still in the mood of the soliloquy; he is indulging his taste for developing abstract ideas at rather tiresome length. The speech demonstrates his high-mindedness, but is hardly calculated to fire his followers with enthusiasm. In all probability they wait with what courtesy they can muster till the flow stops, without attempting to follow it at all.

148 *youths* youth. In modern English the abstract noun is not used in the plural.

150 *break with* break silence to, therefore disclose our plans to. Note again a difference of opinion, also how enthusiastically the conspirators supported Cassius, and how quickly they change their tune when Brutus speaks. Casca follows Cassius; Metellus gave a very good reason for wanting Cicero in, and he now remains silent; is he feeling put out because his view has been so summarily overruled?

So let high-sighted tyranny range on,
Till each man drop by lottery. But if these,
As I am sure they do, bear fire enough   *120*
To kindle cowards and to steel with valour
The melting spirits of women, then, countrymen,
What need we any spur but our own cause,
To prick us to redress? What other bond
Than secret Romans, that have spoke the word,   *125*
And will not palter? And what other oath
Than honesty to honesty engaged,
That this shall be, or we will fall for it?
Swear priests and cowards and men cautelous,
Old feeble carrions and such suffering souls   *130*
That welcome wrongs; unto bad causes swear
Such creatures as men doubt; but do not stain
The even virtue of our enterprise,
Nor the insuppressive mettle of our spirits,
To think that or our cause or our performance   *135*
Did need an oath; when every drop of blood
That every Roman bears, and nobly bears,
Is guilty of a several bastardy,
If he do break the smallest particle
Of any promise that hath passed from him.   *140*
CASSIUS: But what of Cicero? Shall we sound him?
    I think he will stand very strong with us.
CASCA: Let us not leave him out.
CINNA: No, by no means.
METELLUS: O, let us have him, for his silver hairs
    Will purchase us a good opinion   *145*
    And buy men's voices to commend our deeds.
    It shall be said his judgement ruled our hands;
    Our youths and wildness shall no whit appear,
    But all be buried in his gravity.
BRUTUS: O, name him not; let us not break with him;   *150*
    For he will never follow anything
    That other men begin.
CASSIUS: Then leave him out.

[57]

155 *meet* fitting.

156 *of* by.

157 *of* in.

158 *A shrewd contriver* a crafty strategist.

159 *improve* make the most of.

160 *annoy us all* give us all serious trouble.

162–83 Brutus dismisses Antony in an almost off-hand manner—cf. 1.2.28–9. Most of this speech is concerned with an important exposition of Brutus' attitude to the conspiracy.

164 as though killing him in savage anger, and continuing to show a cold malice (*envy*) afterwards.

166 *Caius* Caius Cassius.

169–70 These words exactly express the attitude of Brutus. Are they equally true of Cassius?

169 *come by* gain possession of, therefore remove from somebody else.

171 *gentle* noble, as in 'gentleman'. A usual complimentary adjective.

173 Brutus looks on the killing of Caesar as an act of sacrifice. His preoccupation with his motive has blinded him to the simple truth that he is proposing to kill a man, the usual term for which is murder. Does it matter why they do it, or how they do it?

175 *subtle* cunning.

176 *servants* the physical powers. Here the term would cover both feelings and hands. Brutus says the conspirators will have to whip themselves up to commit the act, but the fury so stimulated must not be allowed to linger on.

177–8 this will demonstrate that we are motivated by necessity, not malice.

180 *purgers* purifiers.

183 Cassius gave way readily about Cicero; this time he feels obliged to argue; Antony he thinks a much more dangerous proposition.

184 *ingrafted*. A metaphor from horticulture, and a strong one. When one shoot is engrafted into another they then become one plant. Cassius is convinced that Antony's affection for Caesar is deep.

187 *take thought* grieve; be upset.

CASCA: Indeed he is not fit.

DECIUS: Shall no man else be touched but only Caesar?

CASSIUS: Decius, well urged. I think it is not meet   *155*
  Mark Antony, so well beloved of Caesar,
  Should outlive Caesar; we shall find of him
  A shrewd contriver; and you know his means,
  If he improve them, may well stretch so far
  As to annoy us all; which to prevent,   *160*
  Let Antony and Caesar fall together.

BRUTUS: Our course will seem too bloody, Caius Cassius,
  To cut the head off and then hack the limbs,
  Like wrath in death and envy afterwards;
  For Antony is but a limb of Caesar.   *165*
  Let us be sacrificers, but not butchers, Caius.
  We all stand up against the spirit of Caesar,
  And in the spirit of men there is no blood.
  O, that we then could come by Caesar's spirit,
  And not dismember Caesar! But, alas,   *170*
  Caesar must bleed for it. And, gentle friends,
  Let's kill him boldly, but not wrathfully;
  Let's carve him as a dish fit for the gods,
  Not hew him as a carcass fit for hounds.
  And let our hearts, as subtle masters do,   *175*
  Stir up their servants to an act of rage,
  And after seem to chide 'em. This shall make
  Our purpose necessary and not envious;
  Which so appearing to the common eyes,
  We shall be called purgers, not murderers.   *180*
  And for Mark Antony, think not of him;
  For he can do no more than Caesar's arm
  When Caesar's head is off.

CASSIUS: Yet I fear him;
  For in the ingrafted love he bears to Caesar—

BRUTUS: Alas, good Cassius, do not think of him.   *185*
  If he love Caesar, all that he can do
  Is to himself, take thought and die for Caesar.

188 *And that were much he should.* Either, that would be a lot to expect of him, because he is not accustomed to doing anything very serious; or, more venomously, that is something he could very well do. Again we are aware of the patronizing attitude of Brutus to the 'playboy'.

190 *no fear* nothing to fear.

S.D. An anachronism—the Romans had no striking clocks. Shakespeare does not worry about anachronisms if they serve a dramatic purpose effectively. He relies on the audience in the speed of actual performance not to notice the historical inaccuracy. Is he justified?

192 Shakespeare does not follow the Roman method of reckoning the time. Here and throughout, the references to the time of day are such as would be familiar to his audience.

195 Collect evidence for and against this view.

196 *Quite from the main opinion* having utterly renounced the position.

197 *fantasy* fanciful ideas; imagination. *ceremonies* omens, associated with religious rites.

198 *apparent* appearing; which have appeared.

200 *augurers* priests who read the signs and foretell the future.

202 This is typical of Decius, who is a courtier expert in observing the weaknesses of the great and playing on them. There are people who, unable to attain greatness themselves, take malicious glee in pulling the great ones off their pedestals.

204-6 Dangerous animals have each a characteristic vulnerable spot. The unicorn was liable to run his single horn into a tree if his enemy (traditionally the lion) dodged aside; the bear, notoriously slow-witted, was puzzled if brought to face a mirror, and could then be taken off his guard; the elephant would blunder into a hole overlaid with branches; the lion could be led into nets; the most noble animal, man, could likewise be snared —by flattery.

210 *give his humour the true bent* guide his mood in the right direction.

213 *the uttermost* the latest; the limit.

216 *rated* reprimanded; scolded.

218 *by him* to his dwelling.

219 *reasons* reasons for our action.

220 only send him here, and leave me to work on him.

And that were much he should, for he is given
To sports, to wildness, and much company.

TREBONIUS: There is no fear in him; let him not die;   *190*
For he will live, and laugh at this hereafter.   *Clock strikes*

BRUTUS: Peace! Count the clock.

CASSIUS: The clock hath stricken three.

TREBONIUS: 'T is time to part.

CASSIUS: But it is doubtful yet
Whether Caesar will come forth to-day or no;
For he is superstitious grown of late,   *195*
Quite from the main opinion he held once
Of fantasy, of dreams, and ceremonies.
It may be these apparent prodigies,
The unaccustomed terror of this night,
And the persuasion of his augurers,   *200*
May hold him from the Capitol to-day.

DECIUS: Never fear that. If he be so resolved,
I can o'ersway him; for he loves to hear
That unicorns may be betrayed with trees,
And bears with glasses, elephants with holes,   *205*
Lions with toils, and men with flatterers;
But when I tell him he hates flatterers,
He says he does, being then most flattered.
Let me work;
For I can give his humour the true bent,   *210*
And I will bring him to the Capitol.

CASSIUS: Nay, we will all of us be there to fetch him.

BRUTUS: By the eighth hour; is that the uttermost?

CINNA: Be that the uttermost, and fail not then.

METELLUS: Caius Ligarius doth bear Caesar hard,   *215*
Who rated him for speaking well of Pompey;
I wonder none of you have thought of him.

BRUTUS: Now, good Metellus, go along by him;
He loves me well, and I have given him reasons;
Send him but hither, and I'll fashion him.   *220*

CASSIUS: The morning comes upon 's. We'll leave you, Brutus.
And, friends, disperse yourselves; but all remember
What you have said, and show yourselves true Romans.

225 *put on*   disclose.

226–7 but carry off the business like our Roman actors, with no sign of strain and with dignified serenity.

230 *honey-heavy dew of slumber*.   Notice how much meaning is compressed into these words. We talk of being 'heavy' with sleep; here sleep is referred to as dew, which is refreshing, and is said to be like honey, which combines heaviness and sweetness.

231 *figures*   shapes; imaginary things. *fantasies* fancies.

234 *what mean you?*   what do you mean by being here?

240 *arms across*   the attitude associated with solemn thought.

246 *wafture*   wave.

250 *humour*   a passing mood. In medieval times the word was used for any one of the four fluids of the body—blood, phlegm, choler, melancholy. The balance of these fluids was believed to determine one's mood, and to give rise to all indispositions. This idea seems to be in the writer's mind here.

251 *his*   its, as in 1.2.124.

254 *prevailed on your condition*   affected your frame of mind.

255 I should not know you to be Brutus. *my lord* treated as one word, like French 'monsieur', and 'milord'.

BRUTUS: Good gentlemen, look fresh and merrily;
   Let not our looks put on our purposes, 225
   But bear it as our Roman actors do,
   With untired spirits and formal constancy.
   And so good morrow to you every one.

                    Exeunt all but BRUTUS

   Boy! Lucius! Fast asleep? It is no matter;
   Enjoy the honey-heavy dew of slumber. 230
   Thou hast no figures nor no fantasies
   Which busy care draws in the brains of men;
   Therefore thou sleep'st so sound.

               Enter PORTIA

PORTIA: Brutus, my lord!
BRUTUS: Portia, what mean you? Wherefore rise you now?
   It is not for your health thus to commit 235
   Your weak condition to the raw cold morning.
PORTIA: Nor for yours neither. You've ungently, Brutus,
   Stole from my bed; and yesternight at supper
   You suddenly arose, and walked about,
   Musing and sighing, with your arms across; 240
   And when I asked you what the matter was,
   You stared upon me with ungentle looks.
   I urged you further; then you scratched your head,
   And too impatiently stamped with your foot.
   Yet I insisted, yet you answered not, 245
   But with an angry wafture of your hand
   Gave sign for me to leave you. So I did,
   Fearing to strengthen that impatience
   Which seemed too much enkindled, and withal
   Hoping it was but an effect of humour, 250
   Which sometime hath his hour with every man.
   It will not let you eat, nor talk, nor sleep;
   And could it work so much upon your shape
   As it hath much prevailed on your condition,
   I should not know you Brutus. Dear my lord, 255
   Make me acquainted with your cause of grief.

261 *physical*   according to the laws of the body.

262 *unbraced*   cf. 1.3.48. *humours*   moistures. Cf. line 250.

263 *dank*   disagreeably damp.

265 *contagion*   the touch of the night that can transmit disease.

266 *tempt*   challenge. *the rheumy and unpurged air*   the morning air not yet purified by the health-giving sun, and so liable to inflict rheum, i.e. catarrh.

268 *sick offence*   harmful disorder. It is your mind that is upset with some ailment.

271 *charm*   exert all my influence on.

275 *Why you are heavy*   why your heart is heavy; why you are unhappy.

280–3 *the bond of marriage*.   These words introduce a series of legal terms: *excepted*, *sort*, and *limitation*. The bond does not contain any provision for certain secrets to be excluded from the compact, which enjoins husband and wife to share their secrets; *in sort* means in a manner, in a certain way; a *limitation* is a specified period.

285 *in the suburbs*   on the outskirts, instead of in the heart. The suburbs of London were notorious as the places frequented by bad characters.

288–90 These words are very moving in their profound sincerity; they demonstrate the nobility of the affection that Brutus has for Portia.

BRUTUS: I am not well in health, and that is all.

PORTIA: Brutus is wise, and, were he not in health,
  He would embrace the means to come by it.

BRUTUS: Why, so I do. Good Portia, go to bed.   260

PORTIA: Is Brutus sick, and is it physical
  To walk unbraced and suck up the humours
  Of the dank morning? What, is Brutus sick,
  And will he steal out of his wholesome bed,
  To dare the vile contagion of the night,   265
  And tempt the rheumy and unpurged air
  To add unto his sickness? No, my Brutus;
  You have some sick offence within your mind,
  Which, by the right and virtue of my place,
  I ought to know of; and, upon my knees,   270
  I charm you, by my once-commended beauty,
  By all your vows of love, and that great vow
  Which did incorporate and make us one,
  That you unfold to me, your self, your half,
  Why you are heavy, and what men to-night   275
  Have had resort to you; for here have been
  Some six or seven, who did hide their faces
  Even from darkness.

BRUTUS: Kneel not, gentle Portia.

PORTIA: I should not need, if you were gentle Brutus.
  Within the bond of marriage, tell me, Brutus,   280
  Is it excepted I should know no secrets
  That appertain to you? Am I your self
  But, as it were, in sort or limitation,
  To keep with you at meals, comfort your bed,
  And talk to you sometimes? Dwell I but in the suburbs   285
  Of your good pleasure? If it be no more,
  Portia is Brutus' harlot, not his wife.

BRUTUS: You are my true and honourable wife,
  As dear to me as are the ruddy drops
  That visit my sad heart.   290

PORTIA: If this were true, then should I know this secret.
  I grant I am a woman; but withal

295 *Cato.* A highly respected statesman and Stoic philosopher, whom Brutus greatly admired. He was both uncle and father-in-law of Brutus.

299 *strong proof of my constancy* convincing evidence of my strength of mind.

299–302 In Rome, men were lords and masters; women took second place. Portia's notion of the responsibilities of a wife is more modern: she wants to share her husband's problems. But to do this she must prove her superiority over ordinary women. She decides to show therefore that in some ways at least she is the equal of a man, and demonstrates her ability to bear pain. From this she can argue her ability to understand a man's problems. The argument is less than logical, but Portia rightly supposes that Brutus, the Stoic, will be powerfully impressed by her remarkable action. The incident is taken from Plutarch.

304 Portia has insisted all this while on remaining on her knees. Only now, when Brutus gives way to her, does she permit him to raise her to her feet.

307 *construe* explain.

308 *the charactery of my sad brows* what is written on my sad brow; what the lines on my brow mean.

309 who is that who knocks?

312 *how* how now? A general greeting.

313 *Vouchsafe* be good enough to receive. In modern usage the word means 'be good enough to grant'.

314 *chose out* picked out; selected.

315 *kerchief* head covering; worn by Elizabethans when ill.

321 Ligarius could pull off his kerchief as he says this.

322 *Brave.* Not merely 'courageous'. The word can mean both 'making a fine display' and 'fine, excellent'. Here we might say 'splendid'.

323 *exorcist* magician.

324 *mortified* dead. You have raised up my spirit from the dead.

326 *What's to do?* what's to be done? Note the enthusiasm inspired in Ligarius by Brutus. Some commentators think Brutus is admirable, but cold, a man who could be respected but not easily loved, and so not a good leader. Ligarius clearly is glad to follow Brutus. Is his reaction typical, or exceptional?

A woman that Lord Brutus took to wife;
I grant I am a woman; but withal
A woman well-reputed, Cato's daughter.   295
Think you I am no stronger than my sex,
Being so fathered and so husbanded?
Tell me your counsels, I will not disclose 'em.
I have made strong proof of my constancy,
Giving myself a voluntary wound   300
Here, in the thigh. Can I bear that with patience,
And not my husband's secrets?
BRUTUS: O ye gods,
  Render me worthy of this noble wife!   *Knocking within*
  Hark, hark! one knocks. Portia, go in awhile;
  And by and by thy bosom shall partake   305
  The secrets of my heart.
  All my engagements I will construe to thee,
  All the charactery of my sad brows.
  Leave me with haste. [*Exit* PORTIA] Lucius, who's that
     knocks?

                Re-enter LUCIUS *with* LIGARIUS

LUCIUS: Here is a sick man that would speak with you.   310
BRUTUS: Caius Ligarius, that Metellus spake of.
  Boy, stand aside. Caius Ligarius, how?
LIGARIUS: Vouchsafe good morrow from a feeble tongue.
BRUTUS: O, what a time have you chose out, brave Caius,
  To wear a kerchief! Would you were not sick!   315
LIGARIUS: I am not sick, if Brutus have in hand
  Any exploit worthy the name of honour.
BRUTUS: Such an exploit have I in hand, Ligarius,
  Had you a healthful ear to hear of it.
LIGARIUS: By all the gods that Romans bow before,   320
  I here discard my sickness. Soul of Rome!
  Brave son, derived from honourable loins!
  Thou, like an exorcist, hast conjured up
  My mortified spirit. Now bid me run,
  And I will strive with things impossible,   325
  Yea, get the better of them. What's to do?

327 *whole*   sound, healthy.

328 Ligarius promptly rearranges the words of Brutus showing
that he has understood the veiled meaning. Has he had any
previous inkling of what was brewing? Brutus avoids direct
information, but his delicacy seems unnecessary; Ligarius
takes the idea perfectly calmly.

334 *S.D. Thunder.*   We have been allowed to forget the storm
during this scene, which is dominated by Brutus, who is not
associated with noise. But there was lightning, if only occasional,
near the beginning; now a low ominous roll of thunder accom-
panies the reminder of the intended murder, and marks the
change from the meditative home of Brutus to the very different
scene that is to follow. If the next scene follows quickly, as it
should—in Shakespeare's theatre there would be no break—
the thunder should continue, becoming loud just before the
entry of Caesar.

This scene develops the character of Brutus. We see him with
Lucius, and observe his considerate attitude to the boy. Left
alone, he painstakingly works at his problem, carefully suppressing
any personal feeling, trying to be relentlessly logical, seeking truth
through pure reason. This method blinds him to a fundamental
fact—that he is going to commit a crime. The 'faction' enter, and
we see how they defer to him. There are some uncomfortable
clashes between him and Cassius; Brutus gets his way. Then we
see him with his wife, and though he cannot express emotion
freely, we realise that their love for each other is very real and deep,
a love that includes mutual respect. Finally, the short episode with
Ligarius proves that Brutus can inspire loyalty.

Caesar's house

1 *Nor . . . nor*   neither . . . nor.

5 *present*   immediate.

6 *success*   outcome.

9 This is not the best way to manage Caesar. Calphurnia is giving
him orders; Caesar's instinctive reaction is to assert his inde-
pendence by taking the opposite line. This exchange between
man and wife is very different from the one we saw in the last
scene.

10 *shall forth*   shall go forth. The omission of the verb in such
phrases is common.

13 *stood on*   took my ground on; relied on. *ceremonies* omens,
as in 2.1.197.

BRUTUS: A piece of work that will make sick men whole.

LIGARIUS: But are not some whole that we must make sick?

BRUTUS: That must we also. What it is, my Caius,
   I shall unfold to thee, as we are going   *330*
   To whom it must be done.

LIGARIUS: Set on your foot,
   And with a heart new-fired I follow you,
   To do I know not what; but it sufficeth
   That Brutus leads me on.   *Thunder*

BRUTUS: Follow me, then.   *Exeunt*

SCENE TWO

Thunder and lightning. Enter CAESAR *in his
dressing-gown*

CAESAR: Nor heaven nor earth have been at peace to-night.
   Thrice hath Calphurnia in her sleep cried out,
   'Help, ho! They murder Caesar!' Who's within?

Enter a Servant

SERVANT: My lord?

CAESAR: Go bid the priests do present sacrifice,   *5*
   And bring me their opinions of success.

SERVANT: I will, my lord.   *Exit*

Enter CALPHURNIA

CALPHURNIA: What mean you, Caesar? Think you to walk
   forth?
   You shall not stir out of your house to-day.

CAESAR: Caesar shall forth. The things that threatened me *10*
   Ne'er looked but on my back; when they shall see
   The face of Caesar, they are vanished.

CALPHURNIA: Caesar, I never stood on ceremonies,
   Yet now they fright me. There is one within,
   Besides the things that we have heard and seen,   *15*

In Shakespeare's day women did not appear on the stage—their parts were taken by boys apprenticed to theatrical companies, where the craft of acting could be learned from skilled players. The boy, aged about 15, who is shown in a wig playing Calphurnia, could stay with the company when his voice broke and progress through minor male parts to major ones. Very little is known about the boy-actors, but the best of them were certainly accomplished. Shakespeare did not give them much scope in *Julius Caesar*, but he wrote star parts for them in some of his other plays.

Notice Calphurnia's elaborate dressing-gown: splendid costumes were a feature of Elizabethan productions. Caesar is shown here with a beard; such a departure from history would not upset the audience then, so long as Caesar looked sufficiently commanding.

16 Supply 'who' before *Recounts*. *the watch*. Ancient Rome did not have night watchmen in her streets, but they were familiar characters to Elizabethan Londoners.

20 *right form of war* regular battle order.
22 *hurtled* clattered.
25 *beyond all use* beyond anything we are used to; quite extraordinary.
26 Compare the above speech of Calphurnia with the speeches of Portia in the last scene. The two women are very different in character, though both speak with great sincerity and force. Would it be right to say that Calphurnia is more feminine than Portia?
26–7 In these lines and at 34–37, Caesar declares his belief in predestination, a creed which enables him to face danger and death with equanimity.

28 *Yet* despite all these prodigies.

Recounts most horrid sights seen by the watch.
A lioness hath whelped in the streets,
And graves have yawned and yielded up their dead;
Fierce fiery warriors fought upon the clouds
In ranks and squadrons and right form of war,   20
Which drizzled blood upon the Capitol;
The noise of battle hurtled in the air,
Horses did neigh, and dying men did groan,
And ghosts did shriek and squeal about the streets.
O Caesar, these things are beyond all use,   25
And I do fear them.
CAESAR: What can be avoided
Whose end is purposed by the mighty gods?
Yet Caesar shall go forth; for these predictions
Are to the world in general as to Caesar.

[71]

31 *blaze forth* proclaim. The phrase is vivid and appropriate, suggesting brilliant comets in the sky. The Romans indeed had a legend that a comet appeared after Caesar's death.

32-3 The magnificent line 31 inspires Caesar to a memorable answer.

34-37 Caesar claims that it is absurd to attempt to avoid the purpose of the gods, yet he had ordered the augurers to give him a report. Perhaps he has more misgivings than he cares to admit?

41-8 Now he stubbornly interprets the omens to suit his own decision in defiance of the accepted interpretation. Is his resolution hardened by Calphurnia's opposition? Is he really talking naturally now, or is he posturing—playing the great man even to his wife? He keeps on referring to himself in the third person, as he did in 1.2.17. Surely Calphurnia deserves more intimate treatment.

50-4 This time Calphurnia adopts a more effective approach. She pleads with the strong man to make concession to her feminine weakness; this appeal plays up to Caesar's image of himself.

55-6 Caesar, his sense of superiority appeased, graciously acquiesces.

56 *for thy humour* because of your whim. Caesar will 'humour' his wife.

CALPHURNIA: When beggars die, there are no comets seen; *30*
  The heavens themselves blaze forth the death of princes.
CAESAR: Cowards die many times before their deaths;
  The valiant never taste of death but once.
  Of all the wonders that I yet have heard,
  It seems to me most strange that men should fear, *35*
  Seeing that death, a necessary end,
  Will come when it will come.

Re-enter Servant

               What say the augurers?
SERVANT: They would not have you to stir forth to-day.
  Plucking the entrails of an offering forth,
  They could not find a heart within the beast. *40*
CAESAR: The gods do this in shame of cowardice.
  Caesar should be a beast without a heart
  If he should stay at home to-day for fear.
  No, Caesar shall not. Danger knows full well
  That Caesar is more dangerous than he. *45*
  We are two lions littered in one day,
  And I the elder and more terrible;
  And Caesar shall go forth.
CALPHURNIA: Alas, my lord,
  Your wisdom is consumed in confidence.
  Do not go forth to-day; call it my fear *50*
  That keeps you in the house, and not your own.
  We'll send Mark Antony to the Senate House,
  And he shall say you are not well to-day.
  Let me, upon my knee, prevail in this.
CAESAR: Mark Antony shall say I am not well; *55*
  And, for thy humour, I will stay at home.

Enter DECIUS

Here's Decius Brutus; he shall tell them so.
DECIUS: Caesar, all hail! Good morrow, worthy **Caesar**.
  I come to fetch you to the Senate House.

60 *happy* opportune.

65 Unfortunate Calphurnia! She is wrong again. Why can she not keep her mouth shut? She thinks she is safe enough, remembering line 55, but she has not appreciated the significance of line 63; Caesar has thought again about the lying excuse and discarded it in favour of the more characteristic, and indeed stronger, blunt statement.

67 *To be* and yet be.

73 Now it is Caesar's turn to make the mistake of talking too much. If he had stopped at line 72 Decius would have been hard put to it to argue; the account of Calphurnia's dream gives him an opening.

75 *stays* makes me stay.

89 *tinctures* colours; *cognizance* an identifying badge worn by a retainer. These are technical terms in heraldry. *stains* bloodstains. *relics* treasured and revered mementoes, mostly associated with saints. Decius therefore subtly associates Caesar with the mighty leader whom great men clamour to serve, and also with the saint whom men worship.

91 Again, as at lines 41–48, Caesar favours the more agreeable interpretation. The interpretation of Decius, like Calphurnia's plea at lines 50–54, is more agreeable because it stresses the greatness of Caesar.

CAESAR: And you are come in very happy time 60
  To bear my greeting to the Senators,
  And tell them that I will not come to-day.
  Cannot, is false, and that I dare not, falser;
  I will not come to-day. Tell them so, Decius.

CALPHURNIA: Say he is sick.

CAESAR: Shall Caesar send a lie? 65
  Have I in conquest stretched mine arm so far,
  To be afeared to tell greybeards the truth?
  Decius, go tell them Caesar will not come.

DECIUS: Most mighty Caesar, let me know some cause,
  Lest I be laughed at when I tell them so. 70

CAESAR: The cause is in my will: I will not come;
  That is enough to satisfy the Senate.
  But for your private satisfaction,
  Because I love you, I will let you know:
  Calphurnia here, my wife, stays me at home. 75
  She dreamt to-night she saw my statuë,
  Which like a fountain with an hundred spouts
  Did run pure blood; and many lusty Romans
  Came smiling, and did bathe their hands in it.
  And these does she apply for warnings, and portents 80
  Of evils imminent; and on her knee
  Hath begged that I will stay at home to-day.

DECIUS: This dream is all amiss interpreted;
  It was a vision fair and fortunate.
  Your statue spouting blood in many pipes, 85
  In which so many smiling Romans bathed,
  Signifies that from you great Rome shall suck
  Reviving blood, and that great men shall press
  For tinctures, stains, relics, and cognizance.
  This by Calphurnia's dream is signified. 90

CAESAR: And this way have you well expounded it.

DECIUS: I have, when you have heard what I can say—
  And know it now: the Senate have concluded
  To give this day a crown to mighty Caesar.

96–7 *a mock Apt to be rendered* a natural taunt.

101 Decius has now used flattery, appeal to ambition, and the threat most unbearable for a warrior—that men will call him a coward.

102 pardon me for even mentioning such a possibility.

102–3 *my dear dear love To your proceeding* my profound concern for your advancement. Decius is nearly overdoing it now with his 'dear dear'.

104 my affection overcomes my judgement, which would not normally have allowed me to risk offending you.

107 This could be an instruction to Calphurnia, but it seems better to have a servant standing by to whom the order can be given.

113 *ague* fever. The word has two syllables.

114 Cf. 2.1.213. Brutus speaks this line with significance, but of course it is lost on Caesar.

118 The servant should have been standing with the robe for some time; at this point Caesar can take it from him, give the order 'Bid them prepare within', and put on the robe while he continues to speak.

120 Now Caesar has greeted each man personally—a sign of a practised leader.

If you shall send them word you will not come,   95
Their minds may change. Besides, it were a mock
Apt to be rendered, for some one to say,
'Break up the Senate till another time,
When Caesar's wife shall meet with better dreams.'
If Caesar hide himself, shall they not whisper,   100
'Lo, Caesar is afraid'?
Pardon me, Caesar; for my dear dear love
To your proceedings bids me tell you this;
And reason to my love is liable.
CAESAR: How foolish do your fears seem now, Calphurnia!   105
I am ashamed I did yield to them.
Give me my robe, for I will go.

Enter BRUTUS, LIGARIUS, METELLUS, CASCA, TREBONIUS,
CINNA, *and* PUBLIUS

And look where Publius is come to fetch me.
PUBLIUS: Good morrow, Caesar.
CAESAR: Welcome, Publius.
What, Brutus, are you stirred so early too?   110
Good morrow, Casca. Caius Ligarius,
Caesar was ne'er so much your enemy
As that same ague which hath made you lean.
What is't o'clock?
BRUTUS: Caesar, 't is strucken eight.
CAESAR: I thank you for your pains and courtesy.   115

Enter ANTONY

See! Antony, that revels long o'nights,
Is notwithstanding up. Good morrow, Antony.
ANTONY: So to most noble Caesar.
CAESAR: Bid them prepare within.
I am to blame to be thus waited for.
Now, Cinna; now, Metellus; what, Trebonius!   120
I have an hour's talk in store for you.

128 *like . . . same* to be like is not necessarily to be the same; they may be like friends and yet not be in fact friends.

129 *yearns* grieves. Note how this line keeps us aware of the agony Brutus is going through. No other person in the play seems to suffer like this.

This scene affords a most interesting contrast to the Brutus-Portia dialogue. Caesar and Calphurnia certainly love each other, perhaps more violently than Brutus and Portia, but depth of sympathy is lacking. Caesar is slightly amused at his wife. She is more kittenish than Portia, and she has not the insight to handle her husband successfully. She does not speak after line 65; as soon as Caesar has men to talk to he simply ignores her, but for one remark. Shakespeare ignores her too; he does not provide her with an exit, unless lines 107 and 118 refer to her.

A street near the Capitol

Shakespeare gives no indication of the appearance or character of Artemidorus; the producer then can make what he likes of him, so long as he does not make much of him, for he is no more than a passing incident. His scroll is important; his personality is not.

6–7 *Security gives way to conspiracy* over-confidence leaves the way clear for conspiracy.

8 *lover* friend.

12 beyond the range of the fangs of jealousy.

Short though it is, this scene injects considerable excitement into the audience. There has been a leakage: will Artemidorus succeed in informing Caesar? His information is startlingly accurate.

Before the house of Brutus

After line 2 Portia walks up and down, distracted, not looking at Lucius. She turns round and sees him still there, standing in confusion, not understanding what he is meant to do.

Remember that you call on me to-day;
Be near me, that I may remember you.
TREBONIUS: Caesar, I will. [*Aside*] And so near will I be,
  That your best friends shall wish I had been further.   *125*
CAESAR: Good friends, go in, and taste some wine with me;
  And we, like friends, will straightway go together.
BRUTUS: [*Aside*] That every like is not the same, O Caesar,
  The heart of Brutus yearns to think upon!   *Exeunt*

SCENE THREE

Enter ARTEMIDORUS, *reading a scroll*

ARTEMIDORUS: 'Caesar, beware of Brutus; take heed of
  Cassius; come not near Casca; have an eye to Cinna; trust
  not Trebonius; mark well Metellus Cimber; Decius Brutus
  loves thee not; thou hast wronged Caius Ligarius. There is
  but one mind in all these men, and it is bent against Caesar.   *5*
  If thou beest not immortal, look about you. Security gives
  way to conspiracy. The mighty gods defend thee! Thy
  lover,   ARTEMIDORUS.'

Here will I stand till Caesar pass along,
And as a suitor will I give him this.   *10*
My heart laments that virtue cannot live
Out of the teeth of emulation.
If thou read this, O Caesar, thou may'st live;
If not, the Fates with traitors do contrive.   *Exit*

SCENE FOUR

Enter PORTIA *and* LUCIUS

PORTIA: I prithee, boy, run to the Senate House.
  Stay not to answer me, but get thee gone.
  Why dost thou stay?
LUCIUS: To know my errand, madam.

6 *constancy* self-control.

9 Brutus has kept his promise—2.1.305–8.

18 *bustling rumour* confused noise.

20 *Sooth* in truth.

PORTIA: I would have had thee there and here again
    Ere I can tell thee what thou should'st do there.   5
    O constancy, be strong upon my side!
    Set a huge mountain 'tween my heart and tongue!
    I have a man's mind, but a woman's might.
    How hard it is for women to keep counsel!
    Art thou here yet?

LUCIUS: Madam, what should I do?   10
    Run to the Capitol, and nothing else?
    And so return to you, and nothing else?

PORTIA: Yes, bring me word, boy, if thy lord look well,
    For he went sickly forth; and take good note
    What Caesar doth, what suitors press to him.   15
    Hark, boy! What noise is that?

LUCIUS: I hear none, madam.

PORTIA: Prithee, listen well.
    I heard a bustling rumour, like a fray,
    And the wind brings it from the Capitol.

LUCIUS: Sooth, madam, I hear nothing.   20

Enter the Soothsayer

PORTIA: Come hither, fellow. Which way hast thou been?

SOOTHSAYER: At mine own house, good lady.

PORTIA: What is't o'clock?

SOOTHSAYER: About the ninth hour, lady.

PORTIA: Is Caesar yet gone to the Capitol?

SOOTHSAYER: Madam, not yet. I go to take my stand,   25
    To see him pass on to the Capitol.

PORTIA: Thou hast some suit to Caesar, hast thou not?

SOOTHSAYER: That I have, lady. If it will please Caesar
    To be so good to Caesar as to hear me,
    I shall beseech him to befriend himself.   30

PORTIA: Why, know'st thou any harm's intended towards
    him?

37 *void* empty.

42-3 Fearing that Lucius has heard her, Portia tries to explain away the 'enterprise'.

44 *commend me* give my love.
45 *merry* in good spirits.
  This scene builds up the tension still more. Portia is not as able as she imagined to keep a secret. In her present state she may easily give the plot away.

SOOTHSAYER: None that I know will be, much that I fear may
    chance.
    Good morrow to you. Here the street is narrow.
    The throng that follows Caesar at the heels,
    Of Senators, of praetors, common suitors,   *35*
    Will crowd a feeble man almost to death.
    I'll get me to a place more void, and there
    Speak to great Caesar as he comes along.   *Exit*
PORTIA: I must go in. Ay me, how weak a thing
    The heart of woman is! O Brutus,   *40*
    The heavens speed thee in thine enterprise!
    Sure, the boy heard me.—Brutus hath a suit
    That Caesar will not grant. O, I grow faint.—
    Run, Lucius, and commend me to my lord;
    Say I am merry; come to me again,   *45*
    And bring me word what he doth say to thee.
                     Exeunt separately

Rome. Before the Capitol

The easiest way to stage this scene is to have the crowd milling about at first at the front of the stage. At the back a platform runs the whole width; some pillars on it will suggest the Capitol well enough. In the centre is the chair of state which Caesar will occupy about line 25. The approach to this platform is by five or six large steps in front of the chair. When Caesar takes his place some Senators will stand near him; there must also be some men moving about so that the conspirators are not conspicuous as they take up their positions. There is a good deal of bustling and conversation to begin with. Most of the people pay no attention to the first twelve lines of dialogue. The atmosphere is that of a meeting before the platform party have come on.

1 In spite of 1.2.24, Caesar remembers the Soothsayer's words.

3 *schedule* paper.

4 Decius quickly provides a diversion, thrusting Trebonius, who is holding a scroll, forward towards Caesar. We hear no more of this suit.

8 It is ironical that this noble gesture of Caesar should seal his fate. *us ourself.* The 'royal' plural. *served* attended to.

10 *give place* give way. One or two conspirators will take the opportunity to jostle Artemidorus well away from Caesar, making it clear that he will be even more roughly handled if he resists.

If the staging of the introductory note is adopted, at this point we might make most of the conspirators gradually move to the audience's left. Antony can be inconspicuous on the right, with Trebonius edging towards him. Popilius emerges from far left, passes Brutus and Cassius, and casually crosses the stage, meeting Caesar as he goes. Caesar takes his time, chatting easily to various people, and reaches his seat about line 25. He takes a further moment or two surveying the scene. From line 25 or so the conversation gradually subsides as people realise that Caesar is seated.

13–24 This is a dramatic moment. Popilius makes a perfectly natural remark; it would be normal for anybody present to have some 'enterprise' to put before Caesar. But Cassius, with his tremendous secret, is hypersensitive, and ready to read significance into words that mean more to him than they do to the speaker. Even Brutus seems to have some similar edginess, but he recovers his composure at line 22, and the sudden panic is over.

18 *makes to* makes his way to; moves to.

ACT THREE

SCENE ONE

Flourish. Enter CAESAR, BRUTUS, CASSIUS, CASCA, DECIUS,
METELLUS, TREBONIUS, CINNA, ANTONY, LEPIDUS, ARTEMI-
DORUS, POPILIUS, PUBLIUS, *the* Soothsayer, *and others*

CAESAR: [*To the* Soothsayer] The ides of March are come.
SOOTHSAYER: Ay, Caesar, but not gone.
ARTEMIDORUS: Hail, Caesar! read this schedule.
DECIUS: Trebonius doth desire you to o'er-read,
  At your best leisure, this his humble suit. 5
ARTEMIDORUS: O Caesar, read mine first; for mine's a suit
  That touches Caesar nearer. Read it, great Caesar.
CAESAR: What touches us ourself shall be last served.
ARTEMIDORUS: Delay not, Caesar; read it instantly.
CAESAR: What, is the fellow mad?
PUBLIUS: Sirrah, give place. 10
CASSIUS: What, urge you your petitions in the street?
  Come to the Capitol.

        CAESAR *goes up to the Senate House, the rest*
                following

POPILIUS: I wish your enterprise to-day may thrive.
CASSIUS: What enterprise, Popilius?
POPILIUS: Fare you well.
                   Advances to CAESAR
BRUTUS: What said Popilius Lena? 15
CASSIUS: He wished to-day our enterprise might thrive.
  I fear our purpose is discovered.
BRUTUS: Look how he makes to Caesar. Mark him.
CASSIUS: Casca, be sudden, for we fear prevention.
  Brutus, what shall be done? If this be known, 20
  Cassius or Caesar never shall turn back,
  For I will slay myself.

22 *constant* composed.

24 *change* change expression or colour.

28 *presently* now. *prefer* present.

29 *addressed* prepared. The conspirators begin now to close in on Caesar, Casca making for a position on the platform behind him.

Lines 29 and 30 are spoken in a stage whisper—the general noise has died away.

33 *puissant* powerful; redoubtable.

36 these bows and humble obeisances.

38–9 and change original principles into such laws as children might practise; that is, change the most fundamental and inviolable laws into mere caprice.

39 *fond* foolish; so foolish as to think.

40 *rebel blood.* A rebel does not conform to proper authority; Caesar's disposition does not deviate from its proper attitude.

41–2 *thawed . . . true quality . . . melteth fools.* Again the metaphor of metal. Heat causes metal to change its shape; weak men can be changed, but Caesar's nature never alters from its proper character. The recurring imagery of metal is highly appropriate to the stern Roman character.

43 *Low-crooked* bent low. *fawning* cringing.

47–8 Caesar does not admit to any injustice in the banishment of Cimber, and he cannot be persuaded to change his decision without adequate cause; flattery and pleading are of no avail.

51 *repealing* recalling.

52 Note how Brutus here preserves his dignity with his restrained appeal.

54 *freedom of repeal* liberty to be recalled.

BRUTUS: Cassius, be constant.
  Popilius Lena speaks not of our purposes;
  For look, he smiles, and Caesar doth not change.

CASSIUS: Trebonius knows his time; for, look you, Brutus,   **25**
  He draws Mark Antony out of the way.

                          Exeunt ANTONY *and* TREBONIUS

DECIUS: Where is Metellus Cimber? Let him go,
  And presently prefer his suit to Caesar.

BRUTUS: He is addressed; press near and second him.

CINNA: Casca, you are the first that rears your hand.   **30**

CAESAR: Are we all ready? What is now amiss
  That Caesar and his Senate must redress?

METELLUS: Most high, most mighty, and most puissant Caesar,
  Metellus Cimber throws before thy seat
  An humble heart—   *Kneeling*

CAESAR: I must prevent thee, Cimber.   **35**
  These couchings and these lowly courtesies
  Might fire the blood of ordinary men,
  And turn pre-ordinance and first decree
  Into the law of children. Be not fond,
  To think that Caesar bears such rebel blood   **40**
  That will be thawed from the true quality
  With that which melteth fools—I mean, sweet words,
  Low-crooked curtsies and base spaniel-fawning.
  Thy brother by decree is banished.
  If thou dost bend and pray and fawn for him,   **45**
  I spurn thee like a cur out of my way.
  Know, Caesar doth not wrong, nor without cause
  Will he be satisfied.

METELLUS: Is there no voice more worthy than my own,
  To sound more sweetly in great Caesar's ear   **50**
  For the repealing of my banished brother?

BRUTUS: I kiss thy hand, but not in flattery, Caesar;
  Desiring thee that Publius Cimber may
  Have an immediate freedom of repeal.

CAESAR: What, Brutus!

55 Cassius deliberately makes a show of great servility.

57 *enfranchisement* restoration of full rights of citizenship.

58 Caesar is startled to find the support for Cimber so strong. He has given his decision, and some people have had the effrontery to continue to plead; moreover, these people are two of the most eminent Senators, Brutus and Cassius, who should know better than to go on speaking when he has closed the matter. As a result, he permits himself to make the most arrogant speech we have heard from him, which repels us, and makes us lean towards the conspirators at this most crucial moment.

59 if I could bring myself to beg others to change their minds, I would be able to change my own mind when entreated.

60 *constant as the northern star* steady as the Pole Star, round which all the others revolve.

61–2 which has no peer in all the sky in its capacity to remain absolutely stationary.

63 *unnumbered* innumerable.

65 Supply 'that' before *doth*.

67 *apprehensive* endowed with reason. The implication is that men have minds which they can make up; they should therefore abide by decisions which they have taken.

69 that keeps his position, immune from attack. An ironical claim in view of what is about to happen.

71 *it* is in apposition to the noun clause, *that I am he*. It is strictly unnecessary.

74 *Olympus* the high mountain in Greece where the gods were said to live. The idea of lifting Olympus carried a double notion of impossibility (a) because Olympus was such a huge mountain, (b) because moving Olympus meant moving the gods.

75 *bootless* in vain. If Brutus is unsuccessful, what is the sense in anyone else making an attempt?

77 *Et tu, Brute?* Even you, Brutus?

80 *common pulpits* raised platforms in the Forum, or market place, from which speeches were delivered. Shakespeare's audiences were familiar with outdoor pulpits, which were used in Elizabethan London.

85 Note how considerate Brutus is: he spares a thought for the old Senator in the midst of all this turmoil. It is clear from line 90 that Publius is not in the conspiracy, yet he was one of the group who called on Caesar at 2.2.108. The simplest explanation is that he was a friend of the conspirators but was excluded from their confidence in this matter on account of his age.

86 *confounded* stupefied. *mutiny* uproar.

CASSIUS: Pardon, Caesar! Caesar, pardon!   55
  As low as to thy foot doth Cassius fall,
  To beg enfranchisement for Publius Cimber.
CAESAR: I could be well moved, if I were as you;
  If I could pray to move, prayers would move me;
  But I am constant as the northern star,   60
  Of whose true-fixed and resting quality
  There is no fellow in the firmament.
  The skies are painted with unnumbered sparks,
  They are all fire, and every one doth shine;
  But there's but one in all doth hold his place.   65
  So in the world: 't is furnished well with men,
  And men are flesh and blood, and apprehensive;
  Yet in the number I do know but one
  That unassailable holds on his rank,
  Unshaked of motion; and that I am he,   70
  Let me a little show it, even in this—
  That I was constant Cimber should be banished,
  And constant do remain to keep him so.
CINNA: O Caesar—
CAESAR: Hence! Wilt thou lift up Olympus?
DECIUS: Great Caesar—
CAESAR: Doth not Brutus bootless kneel?   75
CASCA: Speak, hands, for me!
                    They stab CAESAR, CASCA *striking the*
                    first blow and BRUTUS *the last*
CAESAR: Et tu, Brute? Then fall, Caesar!   *Dies*
CINNA: Liberty! Freedom! Tyranny is dead!
  Run hence, proclaim, cry it about the streets!
CASSIUS: Some to the common pulpits, and cry out   80
  'Liberty, freedom, and enfranchisement!'
BRUTUS: People and Senators, be not affrighted.
  Fly not; stand still. Ambition's debt is paid.
CASCA: Go to the pulpit, Brutus.
DECIUS: And Cassius too.
BRUTUS: Where's Publius?   85
CINNA: Here, quite confounded with this mutiny.

In reading the play we may make the mistake of concentrating so much on the dialogue that we underestimate the importance of the action. This fine, vigorous treatment of the assassination should help to restore the balance. It is from the production at the Stratford Shakespearian Festival, Ontario, in 1955, directed by Michael Langham. Left to right standing: Douglas Campbell as Casca; Robert Christie as Caesar; Eric House as Metellus Cimber. Left to right kneeling: Lloyd Bochner as Cassius; Douglas Rain as Decius Brutus.

It is a tremendous moment. At line 75 Caesar was conducting affairs as he always did—an able, virile man at the height of his powers. By line 78 he is dead. The action has been dramatically swift, and so overwhelming in its result that we can hardly realize to the full what has happened—the greatest man in the world has fallen, 'in the twinkling of an eye'. There should be a stricken silence while Caesar falls and rolls against the foot of Pompey's statue. Cinna rouses the people with an almost hysterical outburst, Cassius shouts through a rising tide of confused noise, and only with difficulty can Brutus make himself heard.

89 Note the serene confidence of Brutus. He is sure in his own mind that he has complete justification for what he has done. It seems to him quite unthinkable that he will have any difficulty in convincing everybody else.

94 *abide*   pay the penalty for; answer for.

98 *As it were doomsday*   as if it were the Day of Judgement.
   will   wish to; the modern 'would'.

100 *drawing days out*   prolonging life. *stand upon*   are concerned about. This speech is very similar to Caesar's at 2.2.35-7.

101-5 Casca's observation may well be callously cynical, but the response of Brutus is perfectly consistent with his character. Most people would feel this to be an outrageous moment for philosophical theorizing, but Shakespeare's touch is sure; this is the same man who spoke lines 89-91.

105-10 This ceremony was intended to show that the conspirators openly demonstrated their responsibility for Caesar's death, and felt no need for shame. It follows out the idea Brutus clings to that this is a sacrifice, not a murder. He sees the blood as a symbol of purification, but the audience may well see it very differently, and recoil from the spectacle. Incidentally, the prophecy of Calphurnia's dream is fulfilled.

111-14 The audience have the satisfaction of witnessing the fulfilment of this prophecy themselves!

115 *basis*   the pedestal on which the statue stood. *lies along*   lies stretched out.

116 *So oft*   as often.
117 *knot.*   A good term for a tightly bound group.

METELLUS: Stand fast together, lest some friend of Caesar's
  Should chance—
BRUTUS: Talk not of standing. Publius, good cheer!
  There is no harm intended to your person,   *90*
  Nor to no Roman else. So tell them, Publius.
CASSIUS: And leave us, Publius, lest that the people,
  Rushing on us, should do your age some mischief.
BRUTUS: Do so; and let no man abide this deed
  But we the doers.

Re-enter TREBONIUS

CASSIUS: Where is Antony?   *95*
TREBONIUS: Fled to his house amazed.
  Men, wives, and children stare, cry out, and run,
  As it were doomsday.
BRUTUS: Fates, we will know your pleasures.
  That we shall die, we know; 't is but the time
  And drawing days out, that men stand upon.   *100*
CASCA: Why, he that cuts off twenty years of life
  Cuts off so many years of fearing death.
BRUTUS: Grant that, and then is death a benefit;
  So are we Caesar's friends, that have abridged
  His time of fearing death. Stoop, Romans, stoop,   *105*
  And let us bathe our hands in Caesar's blood
  Up to the elbows, and besmear our swords.
  Then walk we forth, even to the market-place,
  And, waving our red weapons o'er our heads,
  Let's all cry, 'Peace, freedom, and liberty!'   *110*
CASSIUS: Stoop then, and wash. How many ages hence
  Shall this our lofty scene be acted over
  In states unborn and accents yet unknown!
BRUTUS: How many times shall Caesar bleed in sport,
  That now on Pompey's basis lies along   *115*
  No worthier than the dust!
CASSIUS: So oft as that shall be,
  So often shall the knot of us be called

121 *most boldest and best.* Doubling the superlative for emphasis was good English in Shakespeare's day.

123 Note the masterly choice of words in this speech. This is not the message of an irresponsible playboy.

127 *royal.* Shakespeare uses this word to indicate the highest nobility. He speaks elsewhere of the 'royal disposition' of the lion.

131 *be resolved* have it made clear.

136 through the dangers of this state of affairs of which we know nothing.

138 Brutus, in whose nature is no guile, never suspects guile in others. The message of Antony to him is thoroughly reasonable. A more suspicious approach would reveal sinister possibilities in Antony's condition—perhaps he will not be so easy to convince as Brutus imagines.

140 *so please him come* if he will be good enough to come.

142 *presently* at once.

143 *well to friend* for a good friend.

145 *still* always.

146 hits the nail on the head.

The men that gave their country liberty.

DECIUS: What, shall we forth?

CASSIUS: Ay, every man away.

  Brutus shall lead, and we will grace his heels   *120*

  With the most boldest and best hearts of Rome.

Enter a Servant

BRUTUS: Soft, who comes here? A friend of Antony's.

SERVANT: Thus, Brutus, did my master bid me kneel;

  Thus did Mark Antony bid me fall down;

  And, being prostrate, thus he bade me say: *125*

  Brutus is noble, wise, valiant, and honest;

  Caesar was mighty, bold, royal, and loving:

  Say I love Brutus, and I honour him;

  Say I feared Caesar, honoured him, and loved him.

  If Brutus will vouchsafe that Antony   *130*

  May safely come to him, and be resolved

  How Caesar hath deserved to lie in death,

  Mark Antony shall not love Caesar dead

  So well as Brutus living; but will follow

  The fortunes and affairs of noble Brutus   *135*

  Thorough the hazards of this untrod state

  With all true faith. So says my master Antony.

BRUTUS: Thy master is a wise and valiant Roman;

  I never thought him worse.

  Tell him, so please him come unto this place,   *140*

  He shall be satisfied; and, by my honour,

  Depart untouched.

SERVANT: I'll fetch him presently.   *Exit*

BRUTUS: I know that we shall have him well to friend.

CASSIUS: I wish we may. But yet have I a mind

  That fears him much; and my misgiving still   *145*

  Falls shrewdly to the purpose.

Re-enter ANTONY

BRUTUS: But here comes Antony. Welcome, Mark Antony.

148 Antony's real interest is in Caesar; he greets the body of Caesar pointedly before he addresses the conspirators.

152 *be let blood* be bled. Elizabethan doctors relied much on the letting of blood for the benefit of the patient. Antony uses the double-edged expression sarcastically. *rank* overgrown, like a luxuriant plant ready for cutting.

154 *nor no* double negative; not uncommon in Shakespeare.

157 *bear me hard* bear ill will towards me.

158 *purpled* stained deep red with blood.

159 *Live* if I were to live.

160 *apt* fit.

161 *mean* means.

Antony is handling a delicate situation. He takes the bold course of sincerity; he does not disguise anything of his affection for Caesar. Brutus characteristically warms to this honesty. Antony also can rely on the promise given by Brutus at lines 141–2.

169 *pitiful* full of pity.

171 *As fire drives out fire.* A proverbial expression in Shakespeare's day. *so pity pity* so pity (for the general wrong of Rome) drives out pity (for Caesar).

174 *malice* power to hurt. Since our hearts are full of brotherly love towards you, our arms, so able (as you see from the blood now on them) to inflict deadly harm upon an enemy, to you are extended in a strong embrace of friendship.

177 *you shall have as much say as anyone.* Note how differently Cassius appeals to Antony. He makes a concrete bargaining offer—power. Brutus remains on a more theoretical plane.

181 *deliver* declare to.

ANTONY: O mighty Caesar! Dost thou lie so low?
  Are all thy conquests, glories, triumphs, spoils,
  Shrunk to this little measure? Fare thee well.   *150*
  I know not, gentlemen, what you intend,
  Who else must be let blood, who else is rank.
  If I myself, there is no hour so fit
  As Caesar's death hour; nor no instrument
  Of half that worth as those your swords, made rich   *155*
  With the most noble blood of all this world.
  I do beseech ye, if you bear me hard,
  Now, whilst your purpled hands do reek and smoke,
  Fulfil your pleasure. Live a thousand years,
  I shall not find myself so apt to die.   *160*
  No place will please me so, no mean of death,
  As here by Caesar, and by you cut off,
  The choice and master spirits of this age.
BRUTUS: O Antony, beg not your death of us.
  Though now we must appear bloody and cruel,   *165*
  As by our hands and this our present act
  You see we do, yet see you but our hands
  And this the bleeding business they have done.
  Our hearts you see not; they are pitiful;
  And pity to the general wrong of Rome—   *170*
  As fire drives out fire, so pity pity—
  Hath done this deed on Caesar. For your part,
  To you our swords have leaden points, Mark Antony;
  Our arms in strength of malice, and our hearts
  Of brothers' temper, do receive you in   *175*
  With all kind love, good thoughts, and reverence.
CASSIUS: Your voice shall be as strong as any man's
  In the disposing of new dignities.
BRUTUS: Only be patient till we have appeased
  The multitude, beside themselves with fear,   *180*
  And then we will deliver you the cause
  Why I, that did love Caesar when I struck him,
  Have thus proceeded.

183 The significant word is *wisdom*, but Antony will allow himself only the faintest emphasis—he must not awaken suspicion in Brutus. He ignores the offer of Cassius. He is not to be trapped into committing himself to any definite undertaking. Does Cassius, the 'keen observer', realise that many of Antony's carefully chosen words have sinister undertones beneath their apparent friendliness? Probably he does; we may therefore imagine his suppressed fury, for Antony persistently treats Brutus as the leader and deals only with him. Brutus, as always, accepts Antony's words at face value.

192 *conceit* conceive; form an opinion of.

196 *dearer* more intensely.

204 *bayed* brought to bay. Not a complimentary figure so far as the conspirators are concerned; the noble animal is brought to bay by a pack of dogs. Antony puns on *hart* and 'heart'. As we have observed (1.1.25) a pun in Shakespeare's day was felt to be appropriate to emphasize emotion.

206 *Signed in thy spoil* bearing the identifying marks of your destruction. *lethe* life blood. Lethe was a stream in the underworld; the departed spirit drank of its waters and forgot his existence in the world. So the word is associated with oblivion; the idea seems to be that as Caesar's life blood flowed away his spirit was carried to oblivion.

211 Again Cassius wants to get down to business.

213 *modesty* moderation.

216 *pricked* have your name ticked on a list.

ANTONY: I doubt not of your wisdom.
Let each man render me his bloody hand.
First, Marcus Brutus, will I shake with you;   *185*
Next, Caius Cassius, do I take your hand;
Now, Decius Brutus, yours; now yours, Metellus;
Yours, Cinna; and, my valiant Casca, yours;
Though last, not least in love, yours, good Trebonius.
Gentlemen all—alas, what shall I say?   *190*
My credit now stands on such slippery ground
That one of two bad ways you must conceit me,
Either a coward or a flatterer.
That I did love thee, Caesar, O, 't is true!
If then thy spirit look upon us now,   *195*
Shall it not grieve thee dearer than thy death
To see thy Antony making his peace,
Shaking the bloody fingers of thy foes,
Most noble! in the presence of thy corse?
Had I as many eyes as thou hast wounds,   *200*
Weeping as fast as they stream forth thy blood,
It would become me better than to close
In terms of friendship with thine enemies.
Pardon me, Julius! Here wast thou bayed, brave hart;
Here didst thou fall; and here thy hunters stand,   *205*
Signed in thy spoil, and crimsoned in thy lethe.
O world, thou wast the forest to this hart;
And this indeed, O world, the heart of thee.
How like a deer, strucken by many princes,
Dost thou here lie!   *210*
CASSIUS: Mark Antony—
ANTONY: Pardon me, Caius Cassius.
The enemies of Caesar shall say this;
Then, in a friend, it is cold modesty.
CASSIUS: I blame you not for praising Caesar so,
But what compact mean you to have with us?   *215*
Will you be pricked in number of our friends,
Or shall we on, and not depend on you?

221 Note the condition: I undertook to be friends with you, provided that you explain satisfactorily why Caesar deserved to die. (Cf. lines 130–7).

223 Brutus cordially agrees. He sees no possible difficulty; **Antony** is bound to see the force of the reasons.

224 so much careful thought has gone into our reasons.

228 *Produce* bring out.

230 *order* ceremony.

231 This proves to be a momentous error, and Cassius, fully realizing it, can contain himself no longer. He pulls Brutus down to the front of the stage and expostulates violently with him. Brutus, unruffled as ever, waves the protest aside, and as Cassius furiously mutters line 243 Brutus returns to Antony, who during this exchange has stood alone, apparently with head bowed in thought, looking keenly under his brows at the speakers—he can guess what is being said. The other conspirators stand away from him, looking uneasily from him to their leaders, aware that the situation is uncomfortable but powerless to make any contribution.

236–7 Brutus is happy to be generous to Antony, and to Caesar; he relies on the reasonableness of the people, the justice of his action, and the idealistic motives of the conspirators. How many mistakes is he making?

238 *protest* declare.

242 *advantage* benefit. The word is a verb.

243 *fall* befall; happen.

246 *devise* think of.

ANTONY: Therefore I took your hands, but was indeed
 Swayed from the point, by looking down on Caesar.
 Friends am I with you all, and love you all,   *220*
 Upon this hope, that you shall give me reasons
 Why and wherein Caesar was dangerous.

BRUTUS: Or else were this a savage spectacle.
 Our reasons are so full of good regard
 That were you, Antony, the son of Caesar,   *225*
 You should be satisfied.

ANTONY: That's all I seek;
 And am moreover suitor that I may
 Produce his body to the market-place,
 And in the pulpit, as becomes a friend,
 Speak in the order of his funeral.   *230*

BRUTUS: You shall, Mark Antony.

CASSIUS: Brutus, a word with you.
[*Aside to* BRUTUS] You know not what you do. Do not
  consent
 That Antony speak in his funeral.
 Know you how much the people may be moved
 By that which he will utter?

BRUTUS: By your pardon.   *235*
 I will myself into the pulpit first,
 And show the reason of our Caesar's death.
 What Antony shall speak, I will protest
 He speaks by leave and by permission,
 And that we are contented Caesar shall   *240*
 Have all true rites and lawful ceremonies.
 It shall advantage more than do us wrong.

CASSIUS: I know not what may fall; I like it not.

BRUTUS: Mark Antony, here, take you Caesar's body.
 You shall not in your funeral speech blame us,   *245*
 But speak all good you can devise of Caesar,
 And say you do't by our permission;
 Else shall you not have any hand at all
 About his funeral. And you shall speak

255 If Brutus could hear this, he would be not only resentful, but also depressed and shocked; cf. 2.1.166.

257 *in the tide of times* in the period of time, as opposed to eternity; therefore, 'in the world' would convey the same idea.

264 *cumber* burden; harass.

265 *in use* usual, commonplace.

269 *with custom of fell deeds* by familiarity with cruel deeds.

270 *ranging* roving.

271 *Até* the goddess of discord.

272 *confines* territory. Antony's vigorous imagination conceives a vision of Caesar's spirit, now free from his body, flying at large, and now descending to the limited territory of Italy to set in train fearful destruction. Lines 262–73, with their tremendous mounting urgency, leave no doubt as to the formidable power of Antony when he really means business.

272–3 *with a monarch's voice Cry 'Havoc!'* This call was a military command that no quarter must be given, and only someone with the authority of a king could give such an order. *let slip the dogs of war* slip the leashes off the heads of the hounds. The dogs of war are famine, sword, and fire.

276 Octavius Caesar was the nephew and adopted son of Julius Caesar.

In the same pulpit whereto I am going,   250
After my speech is ended.
ANTONY: Be it so;
I do desire no more.
BRUTUS: Prepare the body then, and follow us.

                                   Exeunt all but ANTONY

ANTONY: O, pardon me, thou bleeding piece of earth,
That I am meek and gentle with these butchers!   255
Thou art the ruins of the noblest man
That ever lived in the tide of times.
Woe to the hand that shed this costly blood!
Over thy wounds now do I prophesy—
Which, like dumb mouths, do ope their ruby lips   260
To beg the voice and utterance of my tongue—
A curse shall light upon the limbs of men;
Domestic fury and fierce civil strife
Shall cumber all the parts of Italy;
Blood and destruction shall be so in use,   265
And dreadful objects so familiar,
That mothers shall but smile when they behold
Their infants quartered with the hands of war,
All pity choked with custom of fell deeds;
And Caesar's spirit, ranging for revenge,   270
With Até by his side come hot from hell,
Shall in these confines with a monarch's voice
Cry 'Havoc!' and let slip the dogs of war,
That this foul deed shall smell above the earth
With carrion men, groaning for burial.   275

Enter a Servant

You serve Octavius Caesar, do you not?
SERVANT: I do, Mark Antony.
ANTONY: Caesar did write for him to come to Rome.
SERVANT: He did receive his letters, and is coming,
And bid me say to you by word of mouth—   280
O Caesar!   *Seeing the body*

282 *big* swelling with grief.
283 *Passion* emotion. *catching* infectious.

286 A league is three miles.
287 *Post* travel with the utmost speed.

289 *Rome* again the pun on 'Rome' and 'room'.
290 *Hie* hurry.
291 *back* go back.

294 *issue* action.

The Forum

As at the beginning of 1.1 the crowd are noisy and unruly, but now they are puzzled and angry, not festive. They are clamouring round Brutus and Cassius, and if they are not soon satisfied they are clearly going to become dangerous.

2 *give me audience* listen to me.

9 Shakespeare has compressed his meaning into an ungrammatical but easily intelligible expression. 'I will hear Cassius, and we can compare their reasons when we have heard them given separately.'
10 *severally* separately. Note that these men declare that they want *reasons*. Brutus provides exactly what they ask; his speech is calm and logical; his whole appeal is to reason.

ANTONY: Thy heart is big; get thee apart and weep.
  Passion, I see, is catching; for mine eyes,
  Seeing those beads of sorrow stand in thine,
  Began to water. Is thy master coming?   285
SERVANT: He lies to-night within seven leagues of Rome.
ANTONY: Post back with speed, and tell him what hath
  chanced.
  Here is a mourning Rome, a dangerous Rome,
  No Rome of safety for Octavius yet;
  Hie hence, and tell him so. Yet, stay awhile;   290
  Thou shalt not back till I have borne this corse
  Into the market-place; there shall I try,
  In my oration, how the people take
  The cruel issue of these bloody men;
  According to the which thou shalt discourse   295
  To young Octavius of the state of things.
  Lend me your hand.   *Exeunt with* CAESAR'S *body*

SCENE TWO

Enter BRUTUS *and* CASSIUS, *and a throng of*
Citizens

CITIZENS: We will be satisfied! Let us be satisfied!
BRUTUS: Then follow me, and give me audience, friends.
  Cassius, go you into the other street,
  And part the numbers.
  Those that will hear me speak, let 'em stay here: 5
  Those that will follow Cassius, go with him;
  And public reasons shall be rendered
  Of Caesar's death.
FIRST CITIZEN: I will hear Brutus speak.
SECOND CITIZEN: I will hear Cassius, and compare their
  reasons,
  When severally we hear them rendered.   10
              Exit CASSIUS, *with some of the* Citizens
              BRUTUS *goes into the pulpit*

11 *noble.* This adjective almost automatically attaches itself to
Brutus; this is how the public invariably think of him.

12–32 This is a fine piece of oratory, carefully constructed, dignified, resonant. It is in prose, because Brutus disdains emotion,
but it is magnificent prose. Note the elaborately balanced state-
ments, developing into climax in lines 23–6, and 26–8. Then
alliteration is used, for adornment and to catch the ear—the
Elizabethan rather than the Roman ear—in a mounting series
of rhetorical questions: base and bondman, rude and Roman,
vile and love. After the climax comes a pause, and the effective
part of the speech is over. It *has* been effective too; the citizens
applaud Brutus with enthusiasm.

13 *lovers* friends. Brutus addresses them first as citizens of
Rome—a patriotic appeal; secondly as fellow-countrymen—
still patriotic, but with the addition that he is one of them;
thirdly as friends—the purely personal approach is last.

16 *Censure* judge.

17 *senses* perception.

29 *rude* rough; uncultured.

35–6 *The question of his death is enrolled* the circumstances concerning his death are recorded.

36 *extenuated* belittled.

37 *enforced* magnified.

THIRD CITIZEN: The noble Brutus is ascended! Silence!
BRUTUS: Be patient till the last.

    Romans, countrymen, and lovers! Hear me for my cause, and be silent, that you may hear. Believe me for mine honour, and have respect to mine honour, that you may believe. Censure me in your wisdom, and awake your senses, that you may the better judge. If there be any in this assembly, any dear friend of Caesar's, to him I say that Brutus' love to Caesar was no less than his. If then that friend demand why Brutus rose against Caesar, this is my answer: Not that I loved Caesar less, but that I loved Rome more. Had you rather Caesar were living, and die all slaves, than that Caesar were dead, to live all free men? As Caesar loved me, I weep for him; as he was fortunate, I rejoice at it; as he was valiant, I honour him; but, as he was ambitious, I slew him. There is tears for his love; joy for his fortune; honour for his valour; and death for his ambition. Who is here so base that would be a bondman? If any, speak; for him have I offended. Who is here so rude that would not be a Roman? If any, speak; for him have I offended. Who is here so vile that will not love his country? If any, speak; for him have I offended. I pause for a reply.
ALL: None, Brutus, none.
BRUTUS: Then none have I offended. I have done no more to Caesar than you shall do to Brutus. The question of his death is enrolled in the Capitol; his glory not extenuated, wherein he was worthy, nor his offences enforced, for which he suffered death.

    Enter MARK ANTONY *and others, with* CAESAR'S *body.*
        Muffled drums

    Here comes his body, mourned by Mark Antony, who, though he had no hand in his death, shall receive the benefit of his dying, a place in the commonwealth, as which of you shall not? With this I depart, that, as I slew my best lover for the good of Rome, I have the same dagger for myself, when it shall please my country to need my death.
ALL: Live, Brutus! Live! Live!

45-52 There is a general commotion now for several lines, and only
one or two phrases can be heard above the confusion of voices.
Of these by far the most important is shouted by the Third
Citizen, who is trying like the rest to pay Brutus the finest
tribute he can think of. But what he in fact does is to show that
Brutus has utterly failed to make his case clear to the crowd.
Brutus does not hear the Third Citizen. We know that because
he continues unperturbed at line 53. On the other hand, Antony
is now on stage. Does he hear the significant words? If so, what
effect will they have on him?

55 *grace* respect.
56 *Tending to* regarding.

60-70 Again there is a general buzz of conversation; again the
Third Citizen makes himself heard. If the lines spoken by the
rest do not come through it is of little importance.

63 *beholding* beholden; obliged.

71 This is almost the same opening as Brutus used, but now the
personal word comes first. Antony's technique calls for attentive
study. He begins on a very subdued note: he is here to bury his
friend, not to praise him. At this stage the crowd strongly
support Brutus; Antony must not do anything to stir them just
now. He genuinely grieves for Caesar; his grief will command
respect; and so he begins speaking as a man mourning for his
friend. His first reference to Brutus is inoffensive; 'the noble
Brutus' is a term any of his hearers might use.

FIRST CITIZEN: Bring him with triumph home unto his house.

SECOND CITIZEN: Give him a statue with his ancestors.

THIRD CITIZEN: Let him be Caesar.

FOURTH CITIZEN: Caesar's better parts
  Shall be crowned in Brutus.

FIRST CITIZEN: We'll bring him to his house with shouts and   *50*
  clamours.

BRUTUS: My countrymen—

SECOND CITIZEN: Peace! Silence! Brutus speaks.

FIRST CITIZEN: Peace, ho!

BRUTUS: Good countrymen, let me depart alone,
  And, for my sake, stay here with Antony.
  Do grace to Caesar's corpse, and grace his speech   *55*
  Tending to Caesar's glories, which Mark Antony,
  By our permission, is allowed to make.
  I do entreat you, not a man depart,
  Save I alone, till Antony have spoke.   *Exit*

FIRST CITIZEN: Stay, ho! and let us hear Mark Antony.   *60*

THIRD CITIZEN: Let him go up into the public chair.
  We'll hear him. Noble Antony, go up.

ANTONY: For Brutus' sake I am beholding to you.

                        Goes into the pulpit

FOURTH CITIZEN: What does he say of Brutus?

THIRD CITIZEN: He says, for Brutus' sake
  He finds himself beholding to us all.   *65*

FOURTH CITIZEN: 'T were best he speak no harm of Brutus
  here.

FIRST CITIZEN: This Caesar was a tyrant.

THIRD CITIZEN: Nay, that's certain.
  We are blest that Rome is rid of him.

SECOND CITIZEN: Peace! Let us hear what Antony can say.

ANTONY: You gentle Romans—

CITIZENS: Peace, ho! Let us hear him.   *70*

ANTONY: Friends, Romans, countrymen, lend me your ears;
  I come to bury Caesar, not to praise him.
  The evil that men do lives after them;
  The good is oft interred with their bones;

78 *answered it*   answered for it; paid the price. This comment seems fair enough.

87 *the general coffers*   the national treasury. Here the first seed of doubt is sown.

93 *on the Lupercal*   on the day of the Lupercalia—1.1.69.

101 *to mourn*   from mourning. Again, the crowd must concede that this is not unreasonable.
105 He chooses a good point at which to break off. His emotion is real, but at the same time Antony is using it with conscious art. Now the crowd can go over what he has said so far, and he can listen to the comments and judge his next move. He will not make the mistake of pressing on too fast. He stands with head bowed, perhaps hidden in his robe, but he is listening to the reactions of the people.
106–15 Each of these comments will give Antony satisfaction.
106 This is exactly what Antony wanted. He has so far posed as a *reasonable* person, while in fact he has been playing on emotions.
107 This person is won over already.
109 This one goes a step further: he is looking ahead, with misgiving.

So let it be with Caesar. The noble Brutus   75
Hath told you Caesar was ambitious.
If it were so, it was a grievous fault;
And grievously hath Caesar answered it.
Here, under leave of Brutus and the rest—
For Brutus is an honourable man;   80
So are they all, all honourable men—
Come I to speak in Caesar's funeral.
He was my friend, faithful and just to me;
But Brutus says he was ambitious,
And Brutus is an honourable man.   85
He hath brought many captives home to Rome,
Whose ransoms did the general coffers fill;
Did this in Caesar seem ambitious?
When that the poor have cried, Caesar hath wept;
Ambition should be made of sterner stuff.   90
Yet Brutus says he was ambitious,
And Brutus is an honourable man.
You all did see that on the Lupercal
I thrice presented him a kingly crown,
Which he did thrice refuse. Was this ambition?   95
Yet Brutus says he was ambitious,
And sure he is an honourable man.
I speak not to disprove what Brutus spoke,
But here I am to speak what I do know.
You all did love him once, not without cause;   100
What cause withholds you, then, to mourn for him?
O judgement! Thou art fled to brutish beasts,
And men have lost their reason! Bear with me;
My heart is in the coffin there with Caesar,
And I must pause till it come back to me.   105

FIRST CITIZEN: Methinks there is much reason in his sayings.

SECOND CITIZEN: If thou consider rightly of the matter,
Caesar has had great wrong.

THIRD CITIZEN: Has he, masters?
I fear there will a worse come in his place.

[111]

Inacrenism

110 The emphasis is again on *reason*.

112 Now comes a hint of readiness for vengeance. *will dear abide it* will pay dearly for it.

113 Surely it is a woman speaking? Cf. 1.2.268–70. The appeal to emotion has gone home.

114 Note the adjective: Antony has replaced Brutus.

116 *But yesterday* only yesterday. Now the pace of the speech quickens.

118 no one is poor enough to pay him respect, i.e., you are all too high and mighty to pay him respect.

119 Antony is adept at this trick—doing exactly the opposite of what he is professing.

122 Now the word 'honourable' can be spat out, and the crowd begin to growl.

123–5 Antony can now refer to Caesar (the dead), himself, and the crowd as being on one side, and the conspirators on the other.

126 Here Antony introduces two powerful appeals—to curiosity and to greed. He produces a scroll, but replaces it in his robe almost at once.

127 *closet* study; cf. 2.1.35.

128 *commons* common people.

129 Increasing their curiosity.

131 *napkins* handkerchiefs.

137 The Elizabethans would not feel this pun to be out of place, though it must seem so to a modern audience. The line should be chanted.

140 Cf. 1.1.37.

143 Cf. line 119.

FOURTH CITIZEN: Marked ye his words? He would not take the
    crown;   *110*
  Therefore 't is certain he was not ambitious.
FIRST CITIZEN: If it be found so, some will dear abide it.
SECOND CITIZEN: Poor soul! His eyes are red as fire with
    weeping.
THIRD CITIZEN: There's not a nobler man in Rome than Antony.
FOURTH CITIZEN: Now mark him; he begins again to speak. *115*
ANTONY: But yesterday the word of Caesar might
  Have stood against the world; now lies he there,
  And none so poor to do him reverence.
  O masters, if I were disposed to stir
  Your hearts and minds to mutiny and rage,   *120*
  I should do Brutus wrong, and Cassius wrong,
  Who, you all know, are honourable men.
  I will not do them wrong; I rather choose
  To wrong the dead, to wrong myself and you,
  Than I will wrong such honourable men.   *125*
  But here's a parchment with the seal of Caesar;
  I found it in his closet—'t is his will.
  Let but the commons hear this testament—
  Which, pardon me, I do not mean to read—
  And they would go and kiss dead Caesar's wounds,   *130*
  And dip their napkins in his sacred blood,
  Yea, beg a hair of him for memory,
  And, dying, mention it within their wills,
  Bequeathing it as a rich legacy
  Unto their issue.   *135*
FOURTH CITIZEN: We'll hear the will! Read it, Mark Antony!
ALL: The will, the will! We will hear Caesar's will!
ANTONY: Have patience, gentle friends; I must not read it;
  It is not meet you know how Caesar loved you.
  You are not wood, you are not stones, but men;   *140*
  And, being men, hearing the will of Caesar,
  It will inflame you, it will make you mad.
  'T is good you know not that you are his heirs;
  For, if you should, O, what would come of it?

Here we see Antony as played by Keith Michell in the B.B.C. television production of *The Spread of the Eagle*, a nine-part cycle based on three Roman plays by Shakespeare, on 31st May, 1963. Would you expect the intimacy of television to enhance this scene? Which episodes in *Julius Caesar* are likely to gain by being televised, and which are likely to lose?

Antony first appears as Brutus describes him—a gay, athletic man who savours life to the full. He can adapt himself to any company, and lives with gusto. Later we become aware of other characteristics. He is a master of words, and uses his skill with the utmost unscrupulousness. He plays on the baser side of people—his funeral oration is viciously unfair to Brutus, and he knows it, but relentlessly takes his advantage. He has no scruples about signing away his nephew's life, or about treating Lepidus shamefully. He makes full use of Caesar's will, but never intends to carry out its provisions. He is passionate, capable, formidable. He is certainly not a man of high principle. He weighs up his enemies shrewdly, and uses Brutus' virtues as levers against him. He and Cassius meet on very similar terms, but Antony is the more formidable. He makes one mistake, like Cassius—he underestimates his ally. He no doubt expected the youthful Octavius to follow his lead, but Octavius turns out to be even more masterful than himself, and to his extreme annoyance he finds himself taking orders from the younger man.

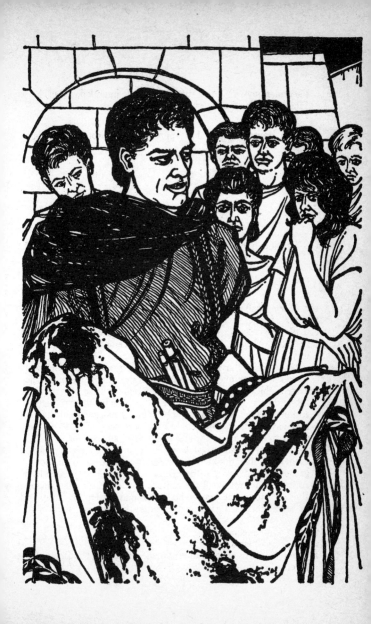

148 *o'ershot myself* gone further than I intended. (Has he?)
This is a figure from archery.

151 The Fourth Citizen has appreciated the irony of 'honourable'.

158–65 Note how eager they are now to please him in every detail.

162 *hearse* coffin on a bier; not the modern meaning.
164 *far* farther.
166 Now that the crowd are completely won over, Antony has no
need to hold back. He takes full advantage of this vital opportunity.
170 *the Nervii* the most formidable warriors of the Belgians.
Caesar's victory over them in 57 B.C. was one of his most celebrated achievements. Antony makes a telling thrust by reminding
his audience of the tremendous celebrations of this victory.
Antony was not with Caesar at this time. But some of his hearers
may have been, for they could have been serving under Caesar,
and if so the reference would affect them all the more.
171–3 Antony's oratory is now in full flood. If the mob were not so
enthralled, they might ask how Antony can identify the various
gashes; if they cared to be cynical, they might even wonder if
Antony had 'improved' the rents for their greater effectiveness.
But as Antony well knows, he has his audience in his hand, and
as he exhibits each gash in the mantle the cries and wails of the
crowd increase.
172 *envious* malicious.
176 *resolved* assured.
178 *angel* a strong term of endearment: his most intimate, best
loved companion.

FOURTH CITIZEN: Read the will! We'll hear it, Antony!   *145*
  You shall read us the will—Caesar's will!
ANTONY: Will you be patient? Will you stay awhile?
  I have o'ershot myself to tell you of it.
  I fear I wrong the honourable men
  Whose daggers have stabbed Caesar; I do fear it.   *150*
FOURTH CITIZEN: They were traitors! Honourable men!
ALL: The will! The testament!
SECOND CITIZEN: They were villains, murderers! The will!
  Read the will!
ANTONY: You will compel me, then, to read the will?
  Then make a ring about the corpse of Caesar,   *155*
  And let me show you him that made the will.
  Shall I descend? and will you give me leave?
ALL: Come down.
SECOND CITIZEN: Descend.
THIRD CITIZEN: You shall have leave.   ANTONY *comes down* 160
FOURTH CITIZEN: A ring! Stand round.
FIRST CITIZEN: Stand from the hearse! Stand from the body.
SECOND CITIZEN: Room for Antony, most noble Antony!
ANTONY: Nay, press not so upon me; stand far off.
ALL: Stand back! Room! Bear back!   *165*
ANTONY: If you have tears, prepare to shed them now.
  You all do know this mantle. I remember
  The first time ever Caesar put it on;
  'T was on a summer's evening, in his tent,
  That day he overcame the Nervii.   *170*
  Look, in this place ran Cassius' dagger through;
  See what a rent the envious Casca made;
  Through this the well-beloved Brutus stabbed,
  And as he plucked his cursed steel away,
  Mark how the blood of Caesar followed it,   *175*
  As rushing out of doors, to be resolved
  If Brutus so unkindly knocked or no;
  For Brutus, as you know, was Caesar's angel.
  Judge, O you gods, how dearly Caesar loved him!

180 *most unkindest*   double superlative, good English in Shake-speare's time.

186 They even accept this without difficulty. The implication would be that the statue miraculously expressed horror, even though Pompey had been Caesar's enemy. A less sensational explanation might be that the statue was splashed with blood. Again we are reminded of Calphurnia's dream.

191 *dint*   impression.

194 Antony has already passed from the appeal of patriotism to the appeal of pity. Now he dramatically whips the mantle from the mangled body of Caesar, and the pity boils over into a furious demand for vengeance.

203 It would seem that Antony's purpose had been accomplished, but he still has some ammunition in reserve.

206-7 This is a typical disclaimer; Antony insists that he has no desire in the world to cause trouble.

208 Now the key-word 'honourable' provokes an angry snarl.

209 Note the grim timing of this sweet reasonable remark. Antony will be able to protest that he stood up for the conspirators. But these apparently sympathetic words spoken at this moment will only inflame the wild mob further, for anything even remotely friendly to the conspirators will meet with violent opposition now.

211 The mob of course will treat this with scorn—what 'reasons' could the conspirators offer against the case of Antony? The irony is that Brutus did in fact give them reasons, which at the time they accepted without reservation.

212-14 This is a very cynical statement. The pose will be popular; crowds always distrust a clever leader, fearing they are being duped. If the leader pretends to be dull—one of *them*—he is more likely to be trusted.

This was the most unkindest cut of all;   *180*
For when the noble Caesar saw him stab,
Ingratitude, more strong than traitors' arms,
Quite vanquished him. Then burst his mighty **heart**;
And in his mantle muffling up his face,
Even at the base of Pompey's statuë,   *185*
Which all the while ran blood, great Caesar fell.
O, what a fall was there, my countrymen!
Then I, and you, and all of us fell down,
Whilst bloody treason flourished over us.
O, now you weep, and I perceive you feel   *190*
The dint of pity. These are gracious drops.
Kind souls, what, weep you when you but behold
Our Caesar's vesture wounded? Look you here!
Here is himself, marred, as you see, with traitors.

FIRST CITIZEN: O piteous spectacle!   *195*

SECOND CITIZEN: O noble Caesar!

THIRD CITIZEN: O woeful day!

FOURTH CITIZEN: O traitors! Villains!

FIRST CITIZEN: O most bloody sight!

SECOND CITIZEN: We will be revenged!   *200*

ALL: Revenge! About! Seek! Burn! Fire! Kill! Slay!
   Let not a traitor live!

ANTONY: Stay, countrymen.

FIRST CITIZEN: Peace there! Hear the noble Antony.

SECOND CITIZEN: We'll hear him, we'll follow him, we'll die
   with him.   *205*

ANTONY: Good friends, sweet friends, let me not stir you up
   To such a sudden flood of mutiny.
   They that have done this deed are honourable.
   What private griefs they have, alas, I know not,
   That made them do it. They are wise and honourable,   *210*
   And will, no doubt, with reasons answer you.
   I come not, friends, to steal away your hearts;
   I am no orator, as Brutus is,
   But, as you know me all, a plain blunt man,

215–16 This is perhaps the most unscrupulous passage in the speech. Antony uses the integrity of Brutus to condemn him. The crowd will readily believe that Brutus would not have taken the risk of allowing a brilliant orator such an opportunity; Brutus did, because he trusted Antony to respect his confidence. Had their places been changed, Brutus would not have treated Antony so basely.

217–18 Typically again, Antony disclaims exactly the powers he has been demonstrating: cleverness, vocabulary, authority, gesture, elocution, compelling power.

219 It is certainly true that he has fluency. But he means that he speaks spontaneously, from the heart, without art or preparation.

222–6 These lines are spoken with unrestrained force—'the power of speech to stir men's blood'.

226 Cf. line 140, and 1.1.37.

235 Cf. line 129.

239 *several* individual. *drachmas.* The drachma was worth about 10d., but it is not possible to suggest a modern equivalent in purchasing power. To humble Romans, however, this would be a substantial bequest.

247 *common pleasures* common pleasure grounds, public parks.

That love my friend; and that they know full well **215**
That gave me public leave to speak of him.
For I have neither wit, nor words, nor worth,
Action, nor utterance, nor the power of speech,
To stir men's blood; I only speak right on.
I tell you that which you yourselves do know, **220**
Show you sweet Caesar's wounds, poor poor dumb mouths,
And bid them speak for me. But were I Brutus,
And Brutus Antony, there were an Antony
Would ruffle up your spirits, and put a tongue
In every wound of Caesar, that should move **225**
The stones of Rome to rise and mutiny.

ALL: We'll mutiny!

FIRST CITIZEN: We'll burn the house of Brutus!

THIRD CITIZEN: Away, then! Come, seek the conspirators!

ANTONY: Yet hear me, countrymen; yet hear me speak. **230**

ALL: Peace, ho! Hear Antony, most noble Antony!

ANTONY: Why, friends, you go to do you know not what.
Wherein hath Caesar thus deserved your loves?
Alas, you know not! I must tell you, then:
You have forgot the will I told you of. **235**

ALL: Most true. The will! Let's stay and hear the will.

ANTONY: Here is the will, and under Caesar's seal.
To every Roman citizen he gives,
To every several man, seventy-five drachmas.

SECOND CITIZEN: Most noble Caesar! We'll revenge his death! **240**

THIRD CITIZEN: O royal Caesar!

ANTONY: Hear me with patience.

ALL: Peace, ho!

ANTONY: Moreover, he hath left you all his walks,
His private arbours, and new-planted orchards, **245**
On this side Tiber; he hath left them you,
And to your heirs for ever—common pleasures,
To walk abroad and recreate yourselves.
Here was a Caesar! When comes such another?

FIRST CITIZEN: Never, never! Come, away, away! **250**

256 *S.D.* The citizens depart in frenzied uproar.

263 *upon a wish* just when I would wish. Shakespeare adapted history here to suit his design; in fact Octavius did not arrive in Rome till six weeks after Caesar's funeral.

267 *Belike* likely, probably.

268 The 'plain, blunt man' has no illusions about his powers!

Look back to the note at the end of 1.1. How many of the mob's characteristics as revealed in that scene are again evident during the speeches of Brutus and Antony?

A street

We have very little evidence in the text of this scene as to the character of Cinna the Poet, but what there is suggests a jaunty fellow who is content to let the rest of the world go by—very unlike the dour politicians to whom public affairs are of consuming interest.

1 *to-night* last night.

2 my imagination is filled with foreboding.

3 *forth* out.

4 *S.D.* The citizens are now a gangster mob spoiling for trouble.

9 *directly* without hedging.

We'll burn his body in the holy place,
And with the brands fire the traitors' houses.
Take up the body.

SECOND CITIZEN: Go fetch fire.

THIRD CITIZEN: Pluck down benches.   255

FOURTH CITIZEN: Pluck down forms, windows, anything.

                              Exeunt Citizens *with the body*

ANTONY: Now let it work. Mischief, thou art afoot,
Take thou what course thou wilt!

                    Enter a Servant

                              How now, fellow!

SERVANT: Sir, Octavius is already come to Rome.

ANTONY: Where is he?   260

SERVANT: He and Lepidus are at Caesar's house.

ANTONY: And thither will I straight to visit him.
He comes upon a wish. Fortune is merry,
And in this mood will give us anything.

SERVANT: I heard him say Brutus and Cassius   265
Are rid like madmen through the gates of Rome.

ANTONY: Belike they had some notice of the people,
How I had moved them. Bring me to Octavius.   *Exeunt*

SCENE THREE

Enter CINNA *the* Poet

CINNA: I dreamt to-night that I did feast with Caesar,
And things unluckily charge my fantasy.
I have no will to wander forth of doors,
Yet something leads me forth.

                    Enter Citizens

FIRST CITIZEN: What is your name?   5

SECOND CITIZEN: Whither are you going?

THIRD CITIZEN: Where do you dwell?

FOURTH CITIZEN: Are you a married man or a bachelor?

SECOND CITIZEN: Answer every man directly.

13 Cinna, pathetically insensitive to the dangerous mood of the crowd, answers cheerfully, almost facetiously.

18 *You'll bear me a bang for that* you'll get a bang for that. The citizens are out for mischief, and the victim cannot win; whatever answer he gives, somebody will take offence.

30 What do they know, or care, about his verses? This brief scene demonstrates the effectiveness of Antony's speech. There is no reason in the people—only a terrifying lust for blood. Cf. 3.2.250–6.

37 *S.D.* Some of the crowd rush off immediately. The rest cluster round Cinna, kill him savagely, and then follow. For a moment we are left looking at the dead body of the Poet sprawled on the stage while the yells of the mob fade away. The curtain falls slowly, as the beginnings of fire flicker across the back-cloth.

In Act 3 we have the climax of the action. Notice the constant changes of atmosphere. Right at the beginning we have the ominous reappearance of the Soothsayer, and of Artemidorus. The conspirators just manage to deal with this critical moment, but before they have time to recover, a casual remark from Popilius shatters their tense nerves again. Once more the tension subsides—all this within twenty-four lines. Then the operation begins. Caesar is provoked into making his most arrogant speech, which indeed has some justification, and is therefore all the more infuriating. At this moment, when he has alienated our sympathy, he is dramatically struck down. In the resultant uproar Brutus remains almost unnaturally composed, and therefore very conspicuous—a lone figure. Antony's messenger enters, and if we listen carefully to him we realize that Antony too is sufficiently in command of himself to frame a masterly message—perhaps we may wonder whether the word 'amazed' in line 96 was a piece of wishful thinking on the part of Trebonius. When Antony himself appears Cassius is almost pushed into the background; again he attempts to influence Brutus in vain. Antony now gives us a foretaste of what is to follow at the funeral, and then we hear for the first time of Octavius Caesar— as one Caesar disappears, another is ready to take his place. The scene which contained the triumph of the conspirators ends on an ominous note for them—as it began. In the second scene the bewildered and therefore dangerous mob are first reassured by Brutus; then Antony, facing a hostile audience, by his tour de force gradually and completely transforms them—how completely we see in the violent third scene.

FIRST CITIZEN: Ay, and briefly.   *10*
FOURTH CITIZEN: Ay, and wisely.
THIRD CITIZEN: Ay, and truly, you were best.
CINNA: What is my name? Whither am I going? Where do
    I dwell? Am I a married man or a bachelor? Then, to
    answer every man directly and briefly, wisely and truly: *15*
    wisely, I say I am a bachelor.
SECOND CITIZEN: That's as much as to say they are fools that
    marry. You'll bear me a bang for that, I fear. Proceed
    directly.
CINNA: Directly, I am going to Caesar's funeral.   *20*
FIRST CITIZEN: As a friend or an enemy?
CINNA: As a friend.
SECOND CITIZEN: That matter is answered directly.
FOURTH CITIZEN: For your dwelling—briefly.
CINNA: Briefly, I dwell by the Capitol.   *25*
THIRD CITIZEN: Your name, sir, truly.
CINNA: Truly, my name is Cinna.
FIRST CITIZEN: Tear him to pieces! He's a conspirator.
CINNA: I am Cinna the poet, I am Cinna the poet.
FOURTH CITIZEN: Tear him for his bad verses! Tear him for his *30*
    bad verses!
CINNA: I am not Cinna the conspirator.
FOURTH CITIZEN: It is no matter, his name's Cinna; pluck but
    his name out of his heart, and turn him going.
THIRD CITIZEN: Tear him, tear him! Come, brands, ho! Fire-   *35*
    brands! To Brutus', to Cassius'! Burn all! Some to Decius'
    house, and some to Casca's; some to Ligarius'. Away, go!
                                                        Exeunt

The meeting of the Triumvirate is shown on the inner stage of the Globe Theatre. The artist has put some effeminate touches into his drawing of Lepidus—the hair style, the soft line of the cheek, the left hand, and the flowing drapery of the toga. Octavius looks like 'a peevish schoolboy', but he has dignity, emphasized by his laurel wreath and royal ermine robe.

Of all the leading characters, Octavius comes nearest to the orthodox conception of a Roman—unimpassioned, disciplined, tight-lipped, confident, masterful, able. In 4.1 he lets Antony make the dangerous decisions, speaking less himself, but keeping the situation clearly in view. Antony talks of jettisoning Lepidus: Octavius observes, 'He's a tried and valiant soldier'. Octavius, good general, has preserved his retreat; if later on there are recriminations, he will say he protested against Antony's action. But he does not definitely refuse to co-operate with Antony; then, if the move is made successfully, he will share the profits. Octavius clearly proposes to look after himself, and is well able to do so. When the leaders meet before the battle he is bored and irritated by the taunting match; he fights with cold steel, not with words. Indeed, cold steel is not a bad description of the man. If he feels any emotion he does not show it. Would Octavius ever permit himself to love a friend as Brutus and Cassius love each other? There is always a barrier between Octavius and Antony; they squabble briefly before the battle, but the lofty decisiveness of Octavius settles the dispute in four syllables—'I will do so.' He properly has the last words in the play, for the future belongs to him. He is the new Caesar in whom the spirit of Julius will survive and continue to rule.

Rome. A room in Antony's house

These three men have taken control of Rome. They are known as the Triumvirate. Lepidus had been Consul along with Julius Caesar in 46 B.C. and was at this time too important to be passed over, but he appears only in this scene, and only for a few lines. Octavius is much younger than Antony, but has an air of authority.

1 *pricked* marked. Cf. 3.1.216.

It is a grim game, bargaining with the lives of men. Lepidus is no match for either of the others; he makes an attempt to assert himself at lines 4–5, but Antony coolly accepts the condition.

6–9 Here we have further light on Antony. He has none of the compunction of Brutus over the shedding of blood; he sends Lepidus on an errand as though he were a servant; and now that the will of Caesar has served his purpose he is quite prepared to 'cut off' some of the legacies that were so influential in swaying the mob in his favour.

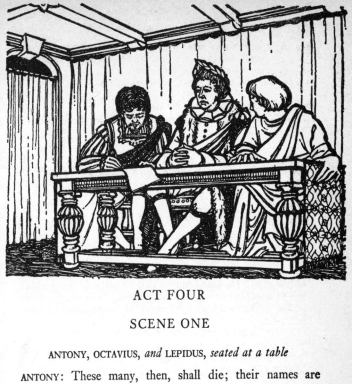

ACT FOUR

SCENE ONE

ANTONY, OCTAVIUS, *and* LEPIDUS, *seated at a table*

ANTONY: These many, then, shall die; their names **are**
  pricked.
OCTAVIUS: Your brother too must die; consent you, Lepidus?
LEPIDUS: I do consent—
OCTAVIUS: Prick him down, Antony.
LEPIDUS: Upon condition Publius shall not live,
  Who is your sister's son, Mark Antony.
ANTONY: He shall not live; look, with a spot I damn him. 5
  But, Lepidus, go you to Caesar's house;
  Fetch the will hither, and we shall determine
  How to cut off some charge in legacies.
LEPIDUS: What, shall I find you here? 10
OCTAVIUS: Or here, or at the Capitol.   *Exit* LEPIDUS

12 *a slight unmeritable man* a nonentity, deserving no respect. Antony reveals his character further; he is prepared to remove Lepidus and so increase his own power.

14 *The three-fold world* Europe, Africa, and Asia.

16 *took his voice* listened to his advice.

17 *black sentence* sentence of death. *proscription* banishment.

20 to relieve ourselves of various burdens of reproach. They will take some unpopular measures, and Lepidus will be made the scapegoat.

27 *in commons* on the common lands. Note that Octavius is a man of few words. He warns Antony that his action is questionable, but he does not oppose it with any vigour. He is therefore conniving at what is going on, but laying the responsibility entirely on Antony.

29 *for that* because of that; for that reason.

32 *wind* wheel, turn.

33 *corporal* bodily, physical.

34 *taste* degree.

37 *abjects, orts* refuse and remnants. He deals in the second-rate.

38 *staled* made cheap; rendered 'stale' by being used too long.

39 *Begin his fashion* appeal to him as novel. The idea is that he is dull and always a step behind other people.

40 *property* a stage term; something that can be brought on stage and used, and then removed again; an inanimate object. Antony and Octavius on the other hand are the actors, persons.

42 *levying powers* enlisting troops. *make head* gather an army.

43 let us combine our forces.

44 let our best friends be made acquainted with our plans, our resources employed to the limit.

45 *presently* at once.

46-7 how hidden dangers may best be discovered, and known dangers most satisfactorily met.

ANTONY: This is a slight unmeritable man,
    Meet to be sent on errands. Is it fit,
    The three-fold world divided, he should stand
    One of the three to share it?

OCTAVIUS: So you thought him,   *15*
    And took his voice who should be pricked to die
    In our black sentence and proscription.

ANTONY: Octavius, I have seen more days than you;
    And though we lay these honours on this man,
    To ease ourselves of divers slanderous loads,   *20*
    He shall but bear them as the ass bears gold,
    To groan and sweat under the business,
    Either led or driven, as we point the way;
    And having brought our treasure where we will,
    Then take we down his load, and turn him off,   *25*
    Like to the empty ass, to shake his ears
    And graze in commons.

OCTAVIUS: You may do your will;
    But he's a tried and valiant soldier.

ANTONY: So is my horse, Octavius; and for that
    I do appoint him store of provender.   *30*
    It is a creature that I teach to fight,
    To wind, to stop, to run directly on,
    His corporal motion governed by my spirit.
    And, in some taste, is Lepidus but so:
    He must be taught, and trained, and bid go forth: *35*
    A barren-spirited fellow; one that feeds
    On abjects, orts, and imitations,
    Which, out of use and staled by other men,
    Begin his fashion. Do not talk of him
    But as a property. And now, Octavius,   *40*
    Listen great things: Brutus and Cassius
    Are levying powers; we must straight make head.
    Therefore let our alliance be combined,
    Our best friends made, our means stretched;
    And let us presently go sit in council   *45*
    How covert matters may be best disclosed,
    And open perils surest answered.

48–9 we are like bears tied to a stake and worried by dogs. Bear-baiting was a popular Elizabethan entertainment.

Act 4 contains the 'falling action'. It presents the dramatist with a real problem—it must be less exciting than Act 3, in order that the climax may remain, as it must, the peak of the action; at the same time, it must not slacken so much that the audience lose interest. The difficulty is beautifully surmounted in this play. First of all we see the effect of the great events of Act 3 on Rome. As we expected after 3.2 and 3.3, the conspirators are not in power. Antony and Octavius have formed a partnership—an interesting parallel to the divided rule on the conspirators' side. The introduction of Octavius at this point is itself a stimulation of interest, especially as we have been prepared for his arrival. Lepidus, the other new character, has also been previously mentioned—once—but he is clearly of less account. Indeed, his brief appearance serves only to enable us to widen our view of the character of Antony. The conference of the new rulers reveals that the citizens are no better off than before. Antony loses no time in examining the will in order to break some of the promises he made at the funeral. There is to be a political purge too. Antony and Octavius show little warmth to each other; their collaboration is convenient, but that is all. Friction is not far away.

Camp near Sardis. Before Brutus' tent

First a drum is heard. At the sound, Brutus and Lucius come out of Brutus' tent, and at the same time Lucilius and Pindarus arrive at the head of a company of soldiers.

6 *He greets me well.* This may mean that Pindarus is an important person to be bringing messages; or perhaps at line 5 Pindarus hands a letter to Brutus which he reads before saying these words.

7 on account of some change in himself, or misled by false counsellors.

8 *worthy* valid.

10 *satisfied* given a full explanation.

12 *full of regard and honour* worthy of all respect and honour.

14 *be resolved* cf. 3.1.131.

16 *familiar instances* signs of friendship.

17 *conference* conversation.

19 Cf. line 7.

21 *enforced ceremony* strained formality.

22 *tricks* deceptions.

23 *hollow* empty, insincere. *hot at hand* eager at first.

OCTAVIUS: Let us do so; for we are at the stake,
  And bayed about with many enemies;
  And some that smile have in their hearts, I fear,   *50*
  Millions of mischiefs.   *Exeunt*

SCENE TWO

Drum. Enter BRUTUS, LUCIUS, LUCILIUS, PINDARUS, *and the
Army*

BRUTUS: Stand, ho!
LUCILIUS: Give the word, ho! and stand.
BRUTUS: What now, Lucilius? Is Cassius near?
LUCILIUS: He is at hand, and Pindarus is come
  To do you salutation from his master.   *5*
BRUTUS: He greets me well. Your master, Pindarus,
  In his own change, or by ill officers,
  Hath given me some worthy cause to wish
  Things done, undone: but, if he be at hand,
  I shall be satisfied.
PINDARUS: I do not doubt   *10*
  But that my noble master will appear
  Such as he is, full of regard and honour.
BRUTUS: He is not doubted. A word, Lucilius;
  How he received you, let me be resolved.
LUCILIUS: With courtesy and with respect enough,   *15*
  But not with such familiar instances
  Nor with such free and friendly conference
  As he hath used of old.
BRUTUS: Thou hast described
  A hot friend cooling. Ever note, Lucilius,
  When love begins to sicken and decay   *20*
  It useth an enforced ceremony.
  There are no tricks in plain and simple faith;
  But hollow men, like horses hot at hand,
  Make gallant show and promise of their mettle;
  But when they should endure the bloody spur,   *25*

26 *fall* let fall. *crests* their arched necks. *jades* worthless creatures.

27 *Sink in the trial* collapse when put to the test.

29 *the horse in general* the main body of cavalry.

34–6 Clearly these words must be called down the line; the Second Soldier must be almost off, or just off the stage, and the Third Soldier should be heard as a distant voice.

37 Cassius is badly upset; he speaks this line with the full force of his anger. For the line to make its maximum impact Cassius and Brutus must be well apart during the quick orders of lines 32–6; then Cassius strides across the stage and hurls line 37 at Brutus as they meet.

40 *sober form* calm, dignified bearing. People think from your appearance that you are incapable of doing wrong.

41 *be content* contain yourself; steady up.

42 *griefs* grievances.

43 It is not practicable to bring whole armies on to the stage. Shakespeare's audience were accustomed to the 'fugleman tradition'—that is, a few soldiers appeared and were understood to be followed by the rest of the troops. On the modern stage the suggestion can be made sufficiently convincing by having noises off, and the men on stage can sometimes turn and look back or exchange a word with those who are following.

46 *enlarge your griefs* express your complaints fully.

48 *their charges* the troops under their command.

52 *S.D.* Though it has become traditional to make a change of scene here in printing the play, on the stage there must be no break. In the Elizabethan theatre Brutus and Cassius would simply move up to the inner stage; a similar effect can be obtained in a modern theatre by playing Scene 2 in front of a traverse curtain and drawing the curtain back at line 52. Brutus and Cassius then move up. How far the interior of the tent has to be indicated by scenery depends naturally on the degree of realism adopted for the whole presentation of the play.

They fall their crests, and like deceitful jades
Sink in the trial. Comes his army on?
LUCILIUS: They mean this night in Sardis to be quartered.
  The greater part, the horse in general,
  Are come with Cassius.

                                        Low march within

BRUTUS: Hark! he is arrived.   *30*
  March gently on to meet him.

          Enter CASSIUS, TITINIUS, *and* Soldiers

CASSIUS: Stand, ho!
BRUTUS: Stand, ho! Speak the word along.
FIRST SOLDIER: Stand!
SECOND SOLDIER: Stand!   *35*
THIRD SOLDIER: Stand!
CASSIUS: Most noble brother, you have done me wrong.
BRUTUS: Judge me, you gods! Wrong I mine enemies?
  And if not so, how should I wrong a brother?
CASSIUS: Brutus, this sober form of yours hides wrongs;   *40*
  And when you do them—
BRUTUS: Cassius, be content;
  Speak your griefs softly; I do know you well.
  Before the eyes of both our armies here,
  Which should perceive nothing but love from us,
  Lest us not wrangle. Bid them move away;   *45*
  Then in my tent, Cassius, enlarge your griefs,
  And I will give you audience.
CASSIUS: Pindarus,
  Bid our commanders lead their charges off
  A little from this ground.
BRUTUS: Lucius, do you the like; and let no man   *50*
  Come to our tent till we have done our conference.
  Lucilius and Titinius, guard our door.   *Exeunt*

Inside Brutus' tent

2 *noted*   branded.

5 *slighted off*   brushed aside.

8 *nice*   slight. That every paltry offence should be solemnly noted.

10 *condemned*   to blame. *an itching palm* a grasping, greedy hand.

11 *mart*   trade.

14 There is no doubting that Cassius is worked up to a killing pitch.

15–16 this would normally be called corruption, but when practised by so great a man as Cassius it must be given a less ugly interpretation, and so the question of punishment does not arise.

20–1 who that touched his body was such a villain that he acted from any other motive than love of justice? Some commentators complain that Brutus has never before mentioned justice as his motive. But surely his argument is clear: that had Caesar become king, injustice would have been rife. This is the republican objection to absolute rule. His point is a telling one, because Cassius was certainly moved at least partly by jealousy.

23 *for supporting robbers.*   This unexpected accusation is not supported by anything else in the play. Shakespeare took it from Plutarch, who declared that Caesar did not himself go in for plundering, but allowed others to do so on his behalf.

25–6 Brutus and Cassius are men of honour; Brutus refers to such honour as vast, and makes a wide sweeping gesture to demonstrate its extent. Then he refers to the contemptible cash for which Cassius would sell his honour and clenches his hand as though grasping coins. *Honours* is plural; his honour and the honour of Cassius. An alternative but less convincing interpretation is that *honours* refers to high offices which they can confer.

27 *bay the moon*   howl at the moon; a proverbial expression.

28 *bay not me*   don't bark at me, like a dog at bear-baiting; cf. 4.1.48–9.

30 *hedge me in*   restrain my freedom. This continues the bear-baiting idea; the dogs formed a ring round the bear.

32 *To make conditions*   to deal with situations; to lay down policy.

SCENE THREE

Enter BRUTUS *and* CASSIUS

CASSIUS: That you have wronged me doth appear in this:
  You have condemned and noted Lucius Pella
  For taking bribes here of the Sardians;
  Wherein my letters, praying on his side,
  Because I knew the man, were slighted off.   *5*

BRUTUS: You wronged yourself to write in such a case.

CASSIUS: In such a time as this it is not meet
  That every nice offence should bear his comment.

BRUTUS: Let me tell you, Cassius, you yourself
  Are much condemned to have an itching palm,   *10*
  To sell and mart your offices for gold
  To undeservers.

CASSIUS: I an itching palm!
  You know that you are Brutus that speak this,
  Or, by the gods, this speech were else your last.

BRUTUS: The name of Cassius honours this corruption,   *15*
  And chastisement doth therefore hide his head.

CASSIUS: Chastisement!

BRUTUS: Remember March, the ides of March remember:
  Did not great Julius bleed for justice' sake?
  What villain touched his body, that did stab,   *20*
  And not for justice? What, shall one of us,
  That struck the foremost man of all this world
  But for supporting robbers, shall we now
  Contaminate our fingers with base bribes,
  And sell the mighty space of our large honours   *25*
  For so much trash as may be grasped thus?
  I had rather be a dog, and bay the moon,
  Than such a Roman.

CASSIUS: Brutus, bay not me!
  I'll not endure it. You forget yourself,
  To hedge me in. I am a soldier, I,   *30*
  Older in practice, abler than yourself
  To make conditions.

35 *Urge* provoke.

36 *health* well-being; safety. *tempt* try.

39 *choler* high temper.

44 *budge* flinch.

45 *Must I observe you?* must I keep a wary eye on you, and fit my behaviour to yours?

46 *testy humour* irritable temper.

47 you shall swallow the poison of your own anger. The spleen was held to be the seat of the passions, particularly anger.

50 *waspish* vicious. Cassius incredulously whispers his words. He is nearly at the end of his tether.

54 *learn of* learn from.

55 Cassius is badly hurt. He genuinely feels that Brutus is being unfair over this.

A. C. Bradley, a most eminent critic, declared the quarrel between Brutus and Cassius to be an 'episode the removal of which would not affect the actual sequence of events', and the comment seems indisputable. Why then did Shakespeare put the quarrel in? Just because it would be 'good theatre'? It certainly is intensely dramatic, and we have plenty of contemporary evidence to prove that the Elizabethans regarded it as a highlight of the play. But that is not its sole justification. Brutus and Cassius appear in this episode not as they are seen by the public, but intimately, as men subject to personal human stresses. Notice too where the quarrel comes in the action of the play: it helps us to understand and sympathize with these men when they are on the brink of momentous action. Our fresh awareness sharpens the poignancy of the doom which falls upon them soon after. Also, after the quarrel Cassius is so shaken that he cannot face the possibility of another clash with Brutus, and defers to Brutus' argument on the question of inviting a pitched battle. This is the decisive error. And the difference of opinion on this crucial

BRUTUS: Go to; you are not, Cassius.

CASSIUS: I am.

BRUTUS: I say you are not.

CASSIUS: Urge me no more, I shall forget myself;   35
Have mind upon your health; tempt me no farther.

BRUTUS: Away, slight man!

CASSIUS: Is't possible?

BRUTUS: Hear me, for I will speak.
Must I give way and room to your rash choler? *anger temper*
Shall I be frighted when a madman stares?   40

CASSIUS: O ye gods, ye gods! must I endure all this?

BRUTUS: All this? Ay, more! Fret till your proud heart **break**!
Go show your slaves how choleric you are,
And make your bondmen tremble. Must I budge?
Must I observe you? Must I stand and crouch   45
Under your testy humour? By the gods,
You shall digest the venom of your spleen,
Though it do split you; for, from this day forth,
I'll use you for my mirth, yea, for my laughter,
When you are waspish.

CASSIUS: Is it come to this?   50

BRUTUS: You say you are a better soldier.
Let it appear so; make your vaunting true,
And it shall please me well. For mine own part,
I shall be glad to learn of noble men.

CASSIUS: You wrong me every way; you wrong me, Brutus. 55
I said, 'an elder soldier,' not 'a better.'
Did I say 'better'?

BRUTUS: If you did, I care not.

CASSIUS: When Caesar lived, he durst not thus have moved
me.

BRUTUS: Peace, peace! You durst not so have tempted him.

CASSIUS: I durst not?   60

BRUTUS: No.

CASSIUS: What? Durst not tempt him?

BRUTUS: For your life you durst not.

[137]

question shows up the fatal weakness in the divided leadership of the conspirators. One of the points that Shakespeare is emphasizing in this play is that people like a hero-leader; remember the Fourth Citizen at 3.2.48. Think too of the devotion of some modern nations to their dictators, and of the British nation to Sir Winston Churchill in the Second World War. Divided rule cannot inspire such loyalty.

Moreover, the quarrel was inevitable; if we look back over the revelation of the two men's characters we see that, despite their very real affection for each other, their differences were bound to lead to a head-on collision sooner or later.

The costumes in this picture are taken from drawings made in 1608 by a Londoner, Thomas Trevelyon, whose picture book, now in the Folger Library in New York, probably shows how Roman characters were dressed on Shakespeare's stage. Brutus stands calmly facing Cassius, whose hand is on his dagger.

64 *that* that which.

68 *idle* ineffective; accomplishing nothing.

69 *respect* pay attention to. This is the climax of the quarrel. Brutus remains so incredibly composed that Cassius gives way before such serene confidence. It is certain that there is no trace of fear in Brutus, even though Cassius has gripped his sword at line 64. Brutus then has the more powerful personality. On the other hand, while we are acknowledging this, do we not recoil from the smugness of line 67?

71 Brutus is surely inconsistent here; he cannot lower himself to acquire money by shady tactics, but if Cassius cares to do so, Brutus is prepared to take the money from him. But Cassius is too broken to take up the point.

75 *indirection* irregularity; wrong methods.

80 *rascal counters* worthless coins. 'Rascal' is a particularly effective word; it meant a deer of no quality, and hunters used 'noble' for its opposite. In addition, it carries the implication of guilt.

65–82 This decisive speech falls into three parts. The first affirms the impregnable confidence of Brutus, the strong tower utterly indifferent to the futile puffs of wind. Cassius must be astonished and mortified to find his attack so contemptuously dismissed, for remember it was Cassius who took the initiative at 4.2.37. The second part of the speech, beginning at line 69, accuses Cassius, again asserts the moral superiority of Brutus, and closes with an emphatic condemnation of unworthy practices. The third part begins like the second, hammering home the point— 'I did send to you for gold, which you denied me'—and ends with an even more determined assertion of integrity.

CASSIUS: Do not presume too much upon my love;
  I may do that I shall be sorry for.
BRUTUS: You have done that you should be sorry for. 65
  There is no terror, Cassius, in your threats,
  For I am armed so strong in honesty
  That they pass by me as the idle wind,
  Which I respect not. I did send to you
  For certain sums of gold, which you denied me; 70
  For I can raise no money by vile means.
  By heaven, I had rather coin my heart,
  And drop my blood for drachmas, than to wring
  From the hard hands of peasants their vile trash
  By any indirection. I did send 75
  To you for gold to pay my legions,
  Which you denied me; was that done like Cassius?
  Should I have answered Caius Cassius so?
  When Marcus Brutus grows so covetous,
  To lock such rascal counters from his friends, 80
  Be ready, gods, with all your thunderbolts;
  Dash him to pieces!

83–4 How true this may have been! A badly delivered message
can cause a lot of mischief. But the idea comes too late—the
damage is done. If Cassius is right about this, the quarrel was
utterly unjustified.

84 *rived*   split, broken.

93 This line touches the keynote of the whole play after the
death of Caesar. The assassination is a crime despite all the fine
talking of Brutus, and Antony and Octavius are the instruments
of retribution. *alone on Cassius* on Cassius alone.

95 *braved*   defied and taunted.

96 *Checked*   rebuked.

97 *conned by rote*   learned by heart.

101 *Plutus*   god of wealth.

103 Cassius is not going back on what he previously said. The
words mean: I, who am believed to have denied thee gold.

106 Brutus has won the day, and can afford to unbend. But his
change of tone here has really been caused by the bitter grief of
Cassius. There were times during the quarrel when Brutus must
have strained the loyalty of his most ardent supporters in the
audience; now that he has permitted himself to be moved by
the plight of his vanquished friend he becomes more human
again. Brutus dislikes emotion, but it is when emotion forces
itself upon him, here and previously, when Portia wrung from
him a declaration of his love for her at 2.1.288, that he is seen at
his best.

107 *it shall have scope*   your anger shall have free play.

108 *dishonour shall be humour*   what would normally be called
dishonourable conduct shall be laughed off as a passing whim.

109–12 Brutus says he is really mild, like a lamb, and anger is not
natural to him. When he does on occasion become angry, the
mood is short-lived, as the spark from a flint is only momentary.

111 *enforced*   forcibly struck.

CASSIUS: I denied you not.

BRUTUS: You did.

CASSIUS: I did not: he was but a fool
That brought my answer back. Brutus hath rived my heart.
A friend should bear his friend's infirmities, 85
But Brutus makes mine greater than they are.

BRUTUS: I do not, till you practise them on me.

CASSIUS: You love me not.

BRUTUS: I do not like your faults.

CASSIUS: A friendly eye could never see such faults.

BRUTUS: A flatterer's would not, though they do appear 90
As huge as high Olympus.

CASSIUS: Come, Antony, and young Octavius, come,
Revenge yourselves alone on Cassius,
For Cassius is aweary of the world; *he's just had enough*
Hated by one he loves; braved by his brother; 95
Checked like a bondman; all his faults observed,
Set in a note-book, learned, and conned by rote,
To cast into my teeth. O, I could weep
My spirit from mine eyes! There is my dagger,
And here my naked breast; within, a heart 100
Dearer than Plutus' mine, richer than gold.
If that thou be'st a Roman, take it forth.
I, that denied thee gold, will give my heart.
Strike as thou didst at Caesar; for, I know,
When thou didst hate him worst, thou lovedst him better 105
Than ever thou lovedst Cassius.

BRUTUS: Sheathe your dagger.
Be angry when you will, it shall have scope;
Do what you will, dishonour shall be humour.
O Cassius, you are yoked with a lamb
That carries anger as the flint bears fire; 110
Who, much enforced, shows a hasty spark,
And straight is cold again.

114 *blood ill-tempered* indisposition. 'Blood' is general physical condition. 'To temper' is 'to mix', and the mixture of the elements in a man determined his 'temperament'. Indispositions were put down to a disturbance of the proper proportions of the elements, or humours.

116–17 These simple words eloquently show the differing characters of the speakers. Brutus is quiet, but affectionate and considerate; Cassius is emotional, controlling himself with difficulty.

119 *rash humour* impetuous temperament.

123–37 The 'poet' who now breaks in has heard the raised voices and is determined to use his good offices to reconcile the commanders. His poetry (lines 130–1) is of no great quality, but his intrusion does have a useful effect, for it makes Cassius laugh, and at once the tension drops. Brutus is less easily amused, and Cassius, more sympathetic, has to put in a plea for indulgence.

124 *grudge* bad feeling.

132 *cynic* crude customer. The Cynics were philosophers who scorned all artistic activity. A cynic therefore would not be much of a poet.

133 *sirrah* sir, but spoken to an inferior.

135 I'll accept his way of carrying on when he chooses a suitable time for it.

136 *jigging fools* silly makers of poor verses. A jig is a lively dance; applied to verses it means that they jump instead of flowing.

137 *Companion* clown—a term of contempt, like our 'fellow'.

CASSIUS: Hath Cassius lived
  To be but mirth and laughter to his Brutus,
  When grief and blood ill-tempered vexeth him?
BRUTUS: When I spoke that, I was ill-tempered too.   *115*
CASSIUS: Do you confess so much? Give me your hand.
BRUTUS: And my heart too.
CASSIUS: O Brutus!
BRUTUS: What's the matter?
CASSIUS: Have not you love enough to bear with me,
  When that rash humour which my mother gave me
  Makes me forgetful?
BRUTUS: Yes, Cassius; and, from henceforth,   *120*
  When you are over-earnest with your Brutus,
  He'll think your mother chides, and leave you so.
POET: [*Within*] Let me go in to see the generals.
  There is some grudge between 'em; 't is not meet
  They be alone.   *125*
LUCILIUS: [*Within*] You shall not come to them.
POET: [*Within*] Nothing but death shall stay me.

Enter Poet, *followed by* LUCILIUS, TITINIUS, *and*
LUCIUS

CASSIUS: How now! What's the matter?
POET: For shame, you generals! What do you mean?
  Love, and be friends, as two such men should be;   *130*
  For I have seen more years, I'm sure, than ye.
CASSIUS: Ha, ha! How vilely doth this cynic rhyme!
BRUTUS: Get you hence, sirrah! Saucy fellow, hence!
CASSIUS: Bear with him, Brutus; 't is his fashion.
BRUTUS: I'll know his humour, when he knows his time.   *135*
  What should the wars do with these jigging fools?
  Companion, hence!
CASSIUS: Away, away, be gone!   *Exit* Poet
BRUTUS: Lucilius and Titinius, bid the commanders
  Prepare to lodge their companies to-night.
CASSIUS: And come yourselves, and bring Messala with you   *140*
  Immediately to us.   *Exeunt* LUCILIUS *and* TITINIUS

144 Brutus, being a Stoic, held that one should not be upset by griefs or unduly elated by joys.

150 *insupportable* unbearable.

151 *Impatient*. There is a confused construction here; 'impatience' would make the grammar correct.

152 *with*. This is another confused construction; 'and' is grammatically correct.

153-4 *for with her death That tidings came* for along with news of her death came that news.

154 *distract* distracted; distraught.

155 *swallowed fire*. Plutarch says that she 'took hot burning coals and cast them into her mouth, and kept her mouth so close that she choked herself'. By Roman standards this was a noble death, fitting for a woman who had the fortitude to give herself a voluntary wound to prove her constancy (2.1.299). Shakespeare, however, by adding that she 'fell distract' seems rather to look back to 2.4. Whether we think that she has risen to a noble height, or that her nerve has given way, her suicide means that in her view the cause of Brutus is lost.

164 *call in question* bring under scrutiny; debate. The four men are going to hold a council of war.

165 Cassius is thinking aloud; Brutus quietly checks him. The others do not hear any of this.

168 *power* force; army.

169 *Bending their expedition* directing their course.

BRUTUS: Lucius, a bowl of wine!   *Exit* LUCIUS

CASSIUS: I did not think you could have been so angry.

BRUTUS: O Cassius, I am sick of many griefs.

CASSIUS: Of your philosophy you make no use,
  If you give place to accidental evils.   *145*

BRUTUS: No man bears sorrow better. Portia is dead.

CASSIUS: Ha? Portia?

BRUTUS: She is dead.

CASSIUS: How 'scaped I killing when I crossed you so?
  O insupportable and touching loss!   *150*
  Upon what sickness?

BRUTUS: Impatient of my absence,
  And grief that young Octavius with Mark Antony
  Have made themselves so strong; for with her death
  That tidings came. With this she fell distract,
  And, her attendants absent, swallowed fire.   *155*

CASSIUS: And died so?

BRUTUS: Even so.

CASSIUS: O ye immortal gods!

Re-enter LUCIUS, *with wine and candles*

BRUTUS: Speak no more of her. Give me a bowl of wine.
  In this I bury all unkindness, Cassius.

CASSIUS: My heart is thirsty for that noble pledge.
  Fill, Lucius, till the wine o'erswell the cup;   *160*
  I cannot drink too much of Brutus' love.   *Exit* LUCIUS

Re-enter TITINIUS, *with* MESSALA

BRUTUS: Come in, Titinius! Welcome, good Messala.
  Now sit we close about this taper here,
  And call in question our necessities.

CASSIUS: Portia, art thou gone?

BRUTUS: No more, I pray you.   *165*
  Messala, I have here received letters,
  That young Octavius and Mark Antony
  Come down upon us with a mighty power,
  Bending their expedition towards Philippi.

170 *of the selfsame tenour*   to the same effect.

180–94 These lines are probably the original version of the revelation of the death of Portia, but they do not agree with the previous conversation of Brutus and Cassius. Probably Shakespeare changed his mind, and on second thoughts decided to cut out this passage and add lines 142–57, and 165. But when the play was printed both the original and the revised versions were included. It would seem best therefore to omit lines 180–94.

195 *to our work alive*   to the work of us who are alive.
196 *presently*   without delay.

200 *offence*   harm.

MESSALA: Myself have letters of the selfsame tenour.   *170*
BRUTUS: With what addition?
MESSALA: That by proscription and bills of outlawry
    Octavius, Antony, and Lepidus
    Have put to death an hundred Senators.
BRUTUS: Therein our letters do not well agree;   *175*
    Mine speak of seventy Senators that died
    By their proscriptions, Cicero being one.
CASSIUS: Cicero one!
MESSALA: Cicero is dead,
    And by that order of proscription.
    [Had you your letters from your wife, my lord?   *180*
BRUTUS: No, Messala.
MESSALA: Nor nothing in your letters writ of her?
BRUTUS: Nothing, Messala.
MESSALA: That, methinks, is strange.
BRUTUS: Why ask you? Hear you aught of her in yours?
MESSALA: No, my lord.   *185*
BRUTUS: Now, as you are a Roman, tell me true.
MESSALA: Then like a Roman bear the truth I tell:
    For certain she is dead, and by strange manner.
BRUTUS: Why, farewell, Portia. We must die, Messala.
    With meditating that she must die once,   *190*
    I have the patience to endure it now.
MESSALA: Even so great men great losses should endure.
CASSIUS: I have as much of this in art as you,
    But yet my nature could not bear it so.]
BRUTUS: Well, to our work alive. What do you think   *195*
    Of marching to Philippi presently?
CASSIUS: I do not think it good.
BRUTUS: Your reason?
CASSIUS: This it is:
    'T is better that the enemy seek us;
    So shall he waste his means, weary his soldiers,
    Doing himself offence, whilst we, lying still,   *200*
    Are full of rest, defence, and nimbleness.

202 *of force*   necessarily.

204 are only putting up a show of friendliness because they have to.

205 *grudged us contribution*   been unwilling to assist us with money, food, etc.

206 *along by them*   through their territory.

208 *new-added*   reinforced.

212 *Under your pardon*   excuse me. As at 3.1.235, when Brutus has determined on a course of action the opposite opinion does not interest him.

219 *Omitted*   if the flood tide is missed.

223 *ventures*   risks; trading vessels risking the perils of the sea. *with your will*   as you wish. Cassius gives in wearily. He cannot face another quarrel, though Brutus has not convinced him.

227 *niggard*   pay, but not in full.

BRUTUS: Good reasons must, of force, give place to better.
    The people 'twixt Philippi and this ground
    Do stand but in a forced affection;
    For they have grudged us contribution.   205
    The enemy, marching along by them,
    By them shall make a fuller number up,
    Come on refreshed, new-added, and encouraged;
    From which advantage shall we cut him off
    If at Philippi we do face him there,   210
    These people at our back.

CASSIUS: Hear me, good brother.

BRUTUS: Under your pardon. You must note beside
    That we have tried the utmost of our friends,
    Our legions are brim-full, our cause is ripe.
    The enemy increaseth every day;   215
    We, at the height, are ready to decline.
    There is a tide in the affairs of men
    Which, taken at the flood, leads on to fortune;
    Omitted, all the voyage of their life
    Is bound in shallows and in miseries.   220
    On such a full sea are we now afloat,
    And we must take the current when it serves,
    Or lose our ventures.

CASSIUS: Then, with your will, go on;
    We'll along ourselves and meet them at Philippi.

BRUTUS: The deep of night is crept upon our talk,   225
    And nature must obey necessity,
    Which we will niggard with a little rest.
    There is no more to say?

CASSIUS: No more. Good night.
    Early to-morrow will we rise, and hence.

BRUTUS: Lucius! [*Re-enter* LUCIUS] My gown. [*Exit* LUCIUS]
    Farewell, good Messala.   230
    Good night, Titinius. Noble, noble Cassius,
    Good night, and good repose.

236 Cassius adopts the position of an inferior; Brutus gently correets him by calling him 'brother'.

240 *knave* lad; not the modern meaning. *thou art o'erwatched* you have been kept awake too long. Notice how considerate Brutus is to Lucius, and to Varro and Claudius a moment later.

246 *raise* rouse.

248 *watch your pleasure* stay awake, ready to do anything you wish.

250 *otherwise bethink me* change my mind.

257 *an't* if it.

CASSIUS: O my dear brother!
This was an ill beginning of the night.
Never come such division 'tween our souls!
Let it not, Brutus.
BRUTUS: Everything is well.   235
CASSIUS: Good night, my lord.
BRUTUS: Good night, good brother.
TITINIUS, MESSALA: Good night, Lord Brutus.
BRUTUS: Farewell, every one.

> *Exeunt* CASSIUS, TITINIUS, *and* MESSALA

> *Re-enter* LUCIUS, *with the gown*

Give me the gown. Where is thy instrument?
LUCIUS: Here in the tent.
BRUTUS: What, thou speak'st drowsily?
Poor knave, I blame thee not; thou art o'erwatched.   240
Call Claudius and some other of my men;
I'll have them sleep on cushions in my tent.
LUCIUS: Varro and Claudius!

> *Enter* VARRO *and* CLAUDIUS

VARRO: Calls my lord?
BRUTUS: I pray you, sirs, lie in my tent and sleep;   245
It may be I shall raise you by and by
On business to my brother Cassius.
VARRO: So please you, we will stand and watch your pleasure.
BRUTUS: I will not have it so; lie down, good sirs;
It may be I shall otherwise bethink me.   250

> VARRO *and* CLAUDIUS *lie down*

Look, Lucius, here's the book I sought for so;
I put it in the pocket of my gown.
LUCIUS: I was sure your lordship did not give it me.
BRUTUS: Bear with me, good boy, I am much forgetful.
Canst thou hold up thy heavy eyes awhile,   255
And touch thy instrument a strain or two?
LUCIUS: Ay, my lord, an't please you.
BRUTUS: It does, my boy.
I trouble thee too much, but thou art willing.

Again the illustration shows a Globe Theatre production. The boy's instrument is an Elizabethan lute, not a Roman lyre. The Ghost of Caesar appears in a shiny black robe and has a chalk-white face, according to the stage convention of the time.

Shakespeare's Julius Caesar is a most interesting character. He is pompous, he talks of himself as a superhuman being, not subject to the natural laws that govern ordinary men; he is 'constant as the northern star', but we see him being tossed backwards and forwards between Calphurnia and Decius, apparently incapable of making a decision for himself. He has a variety of physical defects, including deafness and epilepsy. He defies superstition, yet he commands the augurers to make sacrifice. Shakespeare has therefore been accused of making a fool of Caesar. But Caesar is not merely foolish: he has indisputable power of personality; he dominates the scene whenever he is present, and not only by virtue of his high office. If he were obviously too small for his shoes, people might pay him lip-service, but they would laugh inwardly as they did so and outwardly when his back was turned. Caesar, on the contrary, commands respect. He is a popular leader. He handles power easily. His individual greetings to the conspirators are a mark of a practised chief, and the conquests we hear of testify to his military prowess. Most important, he represents the spirit of imperialism, which was the spirit of his age. This is the invincible element. The irony of his death is that his physical shortcomings go to the grave with his body, but the spirit cannot be killed. Brutus was therefore wishing for the very opposite of what he achieved. This is the significance of the ghost of Caesar which appears to Brutus in his tent. It is indeed the 'spirit of Caesar', and it authoritatively declares that it will rise again at Philippi. Brutus acknowledges its rising, and his complete disillusionment, when he cries, 'O Julius Caesar, thou art mighty yet!'

261 I know young people require sleep.

264 *If I do live.* This thought must be in any soldier's mind when a battle is imminent; the fact that Brutus expresses it, however, adds to the foreboding atmosphere of a scene in which death has been mentioned several times.

S.D. *Music* instrumental music. In this case the instrument would be a lyre. We have no indication of the words of the song. It has become traditional to use 'Orpheus with his lute' from *Henry VIII*.

267 *leaden mace.* The officer laid his mace on the shoulder of of the person he was arresting. 'Leaden' means heavy, an idea naturally associated with sleep.

272 *the leaf.* This is an anachronism. The book in Roman days would be in the form of a scroll.

The restful song (line 266), the boy falling asleep, and the silence as Brutus reads for a minute or two, together with the dimness of the light (line 274) all make the appearance of the Ghost startlingly dramatic.

LUCIUS: It is my duty, sir.

BRUTUS: I should not urge thy duty past thy might; 260
 I know young bloods look for a time of rest.

LUCIUS: I have slept, my lord, already.

BRUTUS: It was well done; and thou shalt sleep again;
 I will not hold thee long. If I do live,
 I will be good to thee.   *Music, and a song* 265
 This is a sleepy tune. O murderous slumber!
 Layest thou thy leaden mace upon my boy,
 That plays thee music? Gentle knave, good night;
 I will not do thee so much wrong to wake thee.
 If thou dost nod, thou break'st thy instrument; 270
 I'll take it from thee; and, good boy, good night.
           He sits down

 Let me see, let me see; is not the leaf turned down
 Where I left reading? Here it is, I think.

    Enter the Ghost of CAESAR

How ill this taper burns! Ha! Who comes here?

276 *monstrous* unnatural. Cf. 1.3.68.

277 *any thing* any real thing.

279 *stare* stand on end.

285 *will* am prepared to.

287 Brutus calls loudly to bring the Ghost back.

306–7 tell him to set his troops in action early, and lead the way.

Scene 1 ended with a hint of friction between Antony and Octavius; in Scenes 2 and 3 we have friction in earnest—the leading conspirators have a fierce quarrel. Ever since Shakespeare's day this scene has been celebrated. It brings the basic differences in character between Brutus and Cassius right out into the open. With which man do you sympathize in this dispute? There is also the pathos of the death of Portia. The quarrel ends in reconciliation. Cassius is exhausted, Brutus compassionate, but commanding. Poor Cassius! He was never given much advancement by Caesar, hence at least some of his jealousy. Now, when the conspiracy he brilliantly planned has succeeded, he finds himself again a follower. Is he fated always to play second fiddle? The reconciled men sit down in council of war; again they differ; again Brutus steam-rollers over Cassius; and Cassius is too weary to argue—he cannot face another quarrel. And so he bites his tongue and his wiser counsel is rejected. Brutus again demonstrates his considerateness to his subordinates Varro, Claudius, and Lucius, the last in particular, for he is frank enough to admit his fault over the lost book and apologizes to his servant. Then comes the portentous Ghost of Caesar—the spirit of Caesar is by no means dead; his personality is still in the air; he is never far from our thoughts. Brutus faces the apparition with great courage and steady nerves, but the very fact that the Ghost appeared shows that Brutus too is still under the shadow of the friend he killed.

I think it is the weakness of mine eyes   275
That shapes this monstrous apparition.
It comes upon me. Art thou any thing?
Art thou some god, some angel, or some devil,
That makes my blood cold and my hair to stare?
Speak to me what thou art.   280
GHOST: Thy evil spirit, Brutus.
BRUTUS: Why comest thou?
GHOST: To tell thee thou shalt see me at Philippi.
BRUTUS: Well; then I shall see thee again?
GHOST: Ay, at Philippi.
BRUTUS: Why, I will see thee at Philippi, then.   *Exit* GHOST 285
    Now I have taken heart thou vanishest.
    Ill spirit, I would hold more talk with thee.
    Boy! Lucius! Varro! Claudius! Sirs, awake!
    Claudius!
LUCIUS: The strings, my lord, are false.   290
BRUTUS: He thinks he still is at his instrument.
    Lucius, awake!
LUCIUS: My lord?
BRUTUS: Didst thou dream, Lucius, that thou so criedst out?
LUCIUS: My lord, I do not know that I did cry.   295
BRUTUS: Yes, that thou didst. Didst thou see anything?
LUCIUS: Nothing, my lord.
BRUTUS: Sleep again, Lucius. Sirrah Claudius!
    Fellow thou, awake!
VARRO: My lord?   300
CLAUDIUS: My lord?
BRUTUS: Why did you so cry out, sirs, in your sleep?
VARRO, CLAUDIUS: Did we, my lord?
BRUTUS: Ay. Saw you anything?
VARRO: No, my lord, I saw nothing.
CLAUDIUS: Nor I, my lord.
BRUTUS: Go and commend me to my brother Cassius;   305
    Bid him set on his powers betimes before,
    And we will follow.
VARRO, CLAUDIUS: It shall be done, my lord.   *Exeunt*

The Plains of Philippi

4 *battles*   army in lines of battle.

5 *warn*   challenge.

7 *I am in their bosoms*   I can see into their minds.

8–9 *They could be content To visit other places*   they would be glad to be elsewhere.

10 *fearful bravery*   a display of bravado covering fear. *face*   bold front.

14 *Their bloody sign of battle*   a red banner, the Roman battle sign.

15 *something to be done*   something is to be done; some action must be taken.

16 *softly*   slowly.

17 *even*   level.

19 *exigent*   important moment.

20 Note the quiet but decisive manner of Octavius. The relationship between Antony and Octavius is still brittle. Antony has to give way to his laconic ally here in much the same way as Cassius succumbed before the mighty assurance of Brutus in the last scene.

S.D. Observe that there are no trumpets; they would not be appropriate to a republican army.

21 *parley*   conference; usually an attempt to settle differences without fighting.

24 let them attack, and we will defend. Emphasize 'we' and 'their'.

25 *Make forth*   go forward.

ACT FIVE

SCENE ONE

Enter OCTAVIUS, ANTONY, *and their* Army

OCTAVIUS: Now, Antony, our hopes are answered.
  You said the enemy would not come down,
  But keep the hills and upper regions;
  It proves not so. Their battles are at hand;
  They mean to warn us at Philippi here,   5
  Answering before we do demand of them.
ANTONY: Tut, I am in their bosoms, and I know
  Wherefore they do it. They could be content
  To visit other places, and come down
  With fearful bravery, thinking by this face   10
  To fasten in our thoughts that they have courage;
  But 't is not so.

Enter a Messenger

MESSENGER: Prepare you, generals!
  The enemy comes on in gallant show;
  Their bloody sign of battle is hung out,
  And something to be done immediately.   15
ANTONY: Octavius, lead your battle softly on,
  Upon the left hand of the even field.
OCTAVIUS: Upon the right hand I; keep thou the left.
ANTONY: Why do you cross me in this exigent?
OCTAVIUS: I do not cross you; but I will do so.   *March* 20

Drum. Enter BRUTUS, CASSIUS, *and their* Army; LUCILIUS,
      TITINIUS, MESSALA, *and others*

BRUTUS: They stand, and would have parley.
CASSIUS: Stand fast, Titinius; we must out and talk.
OCTAVIUS: Mark Antony, shall we give sign of battle?
ANTONY: No, Caesar, we will answer on their charge.
  Make forth; the generals would have some words.   25

26 Octavius gives this order to one of his officers, as he and Antony step forward.

28 The 'parley' quickly becomes a taunting match, and it immediately shows that fighting is inevitable. Octavius, the practical man, is impatient of words; he takes little part in the following exchanges.

29 Brutus says little more; he remains characteristically dignified, confident but restrained.

30 Antony is in his element at this kind of thing; he is easily the best of the four at word-play.

33 Cassius has some of Antony's talent; he manages to get in one or two cutting taunts. The grammar is wrong here. 'We do not yet know where your blows will fall'—we do not know what kind of blows you will give.

34-5 Hybla, a town in Sicily, was famous for the quality of its honey. Cassius means therefore that Antony is an expert at sweet words—words that are suspiciously sweet.

35 Antony easily picks up Cassius' idea and suggests that the words may be dangerous, like the stings of bees.

38 *threat* threaten.

39 The taunting match takes a nasty turn: Antony loses his temper.

41 *showed your teeth like apes* grinned.

47 if my advice had been followed (2.1.155-61).

48 *the cause* to the matter in dispute. Octavius has left Antony to do the talking so far; he does not like this sort of thing. Now he wants to get it over and start fighting.

49 *The proof* the practical test. *cause*, *arguing*, and *proof* are all legal terms.

52 *goes up* goes back into the scabbard.

54 *another Caesar* Octavius himself.

56 Brutus sharply refutes the charge that he and his party are traitors; he denies that they betrayed Rome.

OCTAVIUS: Stir not until the signal.

BRUTUS: Words before blows; is it so, countrymen?

OCTAVIUS: Not that we love words better, as you do.

BRUTUS: Good words are better than bad strokes, Octavius.

ANTONY: In your bad strokes, Brutus, you give good words;   *30*
    Witness the hole you made in Caesar's heart,
    Crying 'Long live! Hail, Caesar!'

CASSIUS: Antony,
    The posture of your blows are yet unknown;
    But for your words, they rob the Hybla bees,
    And leave them honeyless.

ANTONY: Not stingless too?   *35*

BRUTUS: O yes, and soundless too;
    For you have stolen their buzzing, Antony,
    And very wisely threat before you sting.

ANTONY: Villains, you did not so when your vile daggers
    Hacked one another in the sides of Caesar.   *40*
    You showed your teeth like apes, and fawned like hounds,
    And bowed like bondmen, kissing Caesar's feet;
    Whilst damned Casca, like a cur, behind
    Struck Caesar on the neck. O you flatterers!

CASSIUS: Flatterers! Now, Brutus, thank yourself.   *45*
    This tongue had not offended so to-day
    If Cassius might have ruled.

OCTAVIUS: Come, come, the cause. If arguing make us sweat,
    The proof of it will turn to redder drops.
    Look;   *50*
    I draw a sword against conspirators;
    When think you that the sword goes up again?
    Never, till Caesar's three and thirty wounds
    Be well avenged, or till another Caesar
    Have added slaughter to the sword of traitors.   *55*

BRUTUS: Caesar, thou canst not die by traitors' hands,
    Unless thou bring'st them with thee.

OCTAVIUS: So I hope.
    I was not born to die on Brutus' sword.

59 *strain* breed.

60 *honourable* honourably.

61 *peevish* petty. *worthless* unworthy. Octavius was 21.

62 *a masker* one who took part in masques—dramatic entertainments involving dancing in Shakespeare's day. Cf. 1.2.203-4, 2.2.116.

63 *Old Cassius still!* the same old Cassius!

66 *stomachs* appetites (for fighting).

67 let the wind blow, the waves rise, and the ship set out. We must fight, and the opposition will be formidable.

68 *all is on the hazard* we are gambling everything on the fortunes of war.

72 *as* superfluous in modern English.

74-6 Pompey fought the battle of Pharsalia against his own judgement, accepting the advice of his officers, and was disastrously beaten. Cassius had tried to argue against a pitched battle in 4.3. His reference to Pharsalia emphasizes his distrust of the present action.

77 *held Epicurus strong* considered the doctrines of Epicurus to be sound. Epicurus declared that the gods were not interested in human affairs, and therefore he did not believe in omens.

79 *presage* foretell coming events.

80 *our former ensign* our foremost standard.

83 *Who*; the antecedent is *eagles*. *consorted* accompanied.

85 *steads* places. *ravens*, *crows*, and *kites* are all birds of ill omen who feed on carrion flesh. They have replaced the eagles, noble birds, and national emblems of Rome. Therefore it would seem that fortune was formerly smiling on the conspirators, but that the outlook has now changed.

87 *As* as if. *sickly* ill, ready for death.

88 *fatal* bringing death.

BRUTUS: O, if thou wert the noblest of thy strain,
  Young man, thou couldst not die more honourable.   60

CASSIUS: A peevish schoolboy, worthless of such honour,
  Joined with a masker and a reveller!

ANTONY: Old Cassius still!

OCTAVIUS: Come, Antony; away!
  Defiance, traitors, hurl we in your teeth.
  If you dare fight to-day, come to the field;   65
  If not, when you have stomachs.

             Exeunt OCTAVIUS, ANTONY, *and their* Army

CASSIUS: Why, now, blow wind, swell billow, and swim bark!
  The storm is up, and all is on the hazard.

BRUTUS: Ho, Lucilius! Hark, a word with you.

LUCILIUS: [*Standing forth*] My lord?   70

             BRUTUS *and* LUCILIUS *converse apart*

CASSIUS: Messala!

MESSALA: [*Standing forth*] What says my general?

CASSIUS: Messala,
  This is my birth-day; as this very day
  Was Cassius born. Give me thy hand, Messala.
  Be thou my witness that against my will,
  As Pompey was, am I compelled to set   75
  Upon one battle all our liberties.
  You know that I held Epicurus strong,
  And his opinion; now I change my mind,
  And partly credit things that do presage.
  Coming from Sardis, on our former ensign   80
  Two mighty eagles fell, and there they perched,
  Gorging and feeding from our soldiers' hands,
  Who to Philippi here consorted us.
  This morning are they fled away and gone,
  And in their steads do ravens, crows, and kites   85
  Fly o'er our heads and downward look on us,
  As we were sickly prey; their shadows seem
  A canopy most fatal, under which
  Our army lies, ready to give up the ghost.

MESSALA: Believe not so.

90 *I but believe it partly*   I believe it only partly.

92 *constantly*   without flinching.

93 *Even so, Lucilius.*   Brutus has been conferring with Lucilius during the conversation of Cassius and Messala, a little farther back on the stage. Now they are moving forward, and their voices rise.

94 *The gods to-day stand friendly*   may the gods to-day stand friendly.

95 *Lovers*   friends.

96 *rest still incertain*   are always uncertain.

97 let us turn our minds to the worst possibility.

101–8 following the rule of the Stoic philosophy, according to which I condemned Cato's decision to commit suicide—I don't know how to explain it, but I feel it is cowardly and low to cut short the allotted term of life for fear of what may happen—I am determined to summon up my patience and accept my fate as destined by whatever powers on high govern us here on earth below.

110 *Thorough*   through. This is a common Elizabethan form.

111 In spite of his philosophic principles, Brutus is emphatic that he will not permit himself to suffer this disgrace. This is one thing that would move him to break the Stoic rule he has so firmly kept. Brutus therefore, like Cassius at line 78, is forced in this emergency to take another look at his principles, and finds some modification necessary.

CASSIUS: I but believe it partly,   *90*
  For I am fresh of spirit, and resolved
  To meet all perils very constantly.
BRUTUS: Even so, Lucilius.
CASSIUS: Now, most noble Brutus,
  The gods to-day stand friendly, that we may,
  Lovers in peace, lead on our days to age!   *95*
  But since the affairs of men rest still incertain,
  Let's reason with the worst that may befall.
  If we do lose this battle, then is this
  The very last time we shall speak together.
  What are you then determined to do?   *100*
BRUTUS: Even by the rule of that philosophy
  By which I did blame Cato for the death
  Which he did give himself—I know not how,
  But I do find it cowardly and vile,
  For fear of what might fall, so to prevent   *105*
  The time of life—arming myself with patience
  To stay the providence of some high powers
  That govern us below.
CASSIUS: Then, if we lose this battle,
  You are contented to be led in triumph
  Thorough the streets of Rome?   *110*
BRUTUS: No, Cassius, no. Think not, thou noble Roman,
  That ever Brutus will go bound to Rome;
  He bears too great a mind. But this same day
  Must end that work the ides of March begun,
  And whether we shall meet again I know not.   *115*
  Therefore our everlasting farewell take:
  For ever and for ever farewell, Cassius!
  If we do meet again, why, we shall smile;
  If not, why then, this parting was well made.
CASSIUS: For ever and for ever farewell, Brutus!   *120*
  If we do meet again, we'll smile indeed;
  If not, 't is true this parting was well made.

The field of battle

Brutus left the stage at the end of Scene 1; he was indeed the last speaker. Here he comes on again, and speaks in this scene. Now this is contrary to Shakespeare's normal practice. The producer can choose between two ways of handling the situation. Either Brutus goes off in his usual deliberate manner at the end of Scene 1, and then after a pause with no action at all on stage, comes back at high speed, or, soldiers can open Scene 2 with a series of fights, entries, and exits, but with no words spoken.

S.D. *Alarum*   noise of battle, including trumpet calls.
1 *bills*   notes, instructions.
2 *the other side*   the wing commanded by Cassius.
3 *set on*   attack.
4 *cold demeanour*   lack of spirit.
5 *gives*   will give.

Another part of the field

1 *the villains*   his own men.

3 *ensign*   standard bearer.
4 *it*   the standard.

6 *on*   over.

11 *far*   farther. Cf. 3.2.164.

BRUTUS: Why then, lead on. O that a man might know
The end of this day's business ere it come!
But it sufficeth that the day will end,   *125*
And then the end is known. Come, ho! Away!   *Exeunt*

SCENE TWO

Alarum. Enter BRUTUS *and* MESSALA

BRUTUS: Ride, ride, Messala, ride, and give these bills
Unto the legions on the other side.   *Loud alarum*
Let them set on at once, for I perceive
But cold demeanour in Octavius' wing,
And sudden push gives them the overthrow.   5
Ride, ride, Messala; let them all come down   *Exeunt*

SCENE THREE

Alarums. Enter CASSIUS *and* TITINIUS

CASSIUS: O, look, Titinius, look, the villains fly!
Myself have to mine own turned enemy:
This ensign here of mine was turning back;
I slew the coward, and did take it from him.
TITINIUS: O Cassius, Brutus gave the word too early,   5
Who, having some advantage on Octavius,
Took it too eagerly; his soldiers fell to spoil,
Whilst we by Antony are all enclosed.

Enter PINDARUS

PINDARUS: Fly further off, my lord, fly further off!
Mark Antony is in your tents, my lord;   10
Fly, therefore, noble Cassius, fly far off!
CASSIUS: This hill is far enough. Look, look, Titinius!
Are those my tents where I perceive the fire?
TITINIUS: They are, my lord.

19 *with a thought*   as fast as thought.

21 *thick*   cloudy; dim.   *regard*   keep under observation.

23 *S.D.* In the Elizabethan theatre Pindarus would go to the balcony above the inner stage.

25 *his compass*   its complete circuit, its course.

31 *light*   alight, dismount.

37 *Parthia*   a country in western Asia.
38 *swore thee*   made thee swear. *saving of*   saving.

41 *a freeman.*   As a prisoner of war, Pindarus was the personal slave of his conqueror, but became a free man automatically on his master's death.
42 *search*   probe.
43 *hilts*   hilt. Shakespeare usually uses the plural form.

45 The last words of Cassius are addressed to Caesar.

CASSIUS: Titinius, if thou lovest me,
  Mount thou my horse, and hide thy spurs in him,   *15*
  Till he have brought thee up to yonder troops
  And here again, that I may rest assured
  Whether yond troops are friend or enemy.
TITINIUS: I will be here again even with a thought.   *Exit*
CASSIUS: Go, Pindarus, get higher on that hill;   *20*
  My sight was ever thick; regard Titinius,
  And tell me what thou notest about the field.

                                        PINDARUS *ascends the hill*

  This day I breathed first. Time is come round,
  And where I did begin, there shall I end;
  My life is run his compass. Sirrah, what news?   *25*
PINDARUS: [*Above*] O my lord!
CASSIUS: What news?
PINDARUS: Titinius is enclosed round about
  With horsemen, that make to him on the spur;
  Yet he spurs on. Now they are almost on him.   *30*
  Now, Titinius! Now, some light. O, he lights too.
  He's ta'en. [*Shout.*] And, hark! They shout for joy.
CASSIUS: Come down; behold no more.
  O, coward that I am to live so long
  To see my best friend ta'en before my face!   *35*

                        PINDARUS *descends*

  Come hither, sirrah.
  In Parthia did I take thee prisoner;
  And then I swore thee, saving of thy life,
  That whatsoever I did bid thee do,
  Thou shouldst attempt it. Come now, keep thine oath;   *40*
  Now be a freeman; and with this good sword,
  That ran through Caesar's bowels, search this bosom.
  Stand not to answer; here, take thou the hilts,
  And when my face is covered, as 't is now,
  Guide thou the sword. [PINDARUS *stabs him*] Caesar, thou
    art revenged,
                                                                     45
  Even with the sword that killed thee.   *Dies*

Some of Shakespeare's plays are occasionally produced in modern dress to bring out the contemporary element in them, demonstrating that Shakespeare 'was not of an age, but for all time'. Do you think the death of Cassius hits you more forcefully when you see it as in this drawing, made from the production at Her Majesty's Theatre, Carlisle, in 1961, directed by Robert David MacDonald? Cassius was played by Paul Bacon, Pindarus by the negro actor, Kenneth Gardnier.

Cassius is passionate and warm-hearted. He is moved by less exalted motives than Brutus, and therefore is more understandable to most people. Certainly he is jealous of Caesar, and probably has a real grievance against him. Chafing under the dominance of Caesar, he works fiercely for his downfall, only to find himself under the dominance of Brutus. He is the driving force of the conspiracy, but once the murder is committed he recedes. He admires Brutus, and at the same time smiles at his guilelessness. He is clear-sighted enough to recognize the superior prestige of Brutus, and so works hard to recruit him to the faction. No doubt he was confident that as he succeeded in catching his man, so he would succeed in handling him when caught, but there he made his mistake—the figurehead revealed unexpected strength. And so Cassius has the humiliating experience, over and over again, of seeing his correct judgement overborne. Humiliation is particularly bitter for him because he is proud—otherwise he would not be so jealous. He makes much of Caesar's physical defects, and the crowning frustration is the discovery that in killing Caesar he has destroyed the physical man, but not the spirit to which he has given too little thought. In the end he ironically reveals a physical weakness of his own—'My sight was ever thick'—and has to re-examine his Epicurean philosophy, as Brutus re-examines Stoicism.

48 *Durst I have done my will* if I had dared to do as I wished. Pindarus would rather have slain himself than kill his master, but he lacked the courage.

51 *change* exchange (of fortune). Titinius and Messala do not see Cassius at first.

PINDARUS: So, I am free; yet would not so have been,
    Durst I have done my will. O Cassius!
    Far from this country Pindarus shall run,
    Where never Roman shall take note of him.   *Exit* 50

Re-enter TITINIUS *with* MESSALA

MESSALA: It is but change, Titinius; for Octavius
    Is overthrown by noble Brutus' power,
    As Cassius' legions are by Antony.
TITINIUS: These tidings will well comfort Cassius.
MESSALA: Where did you leave him?
TITINIUS: All disconsolate,   55
    With Pindarus, his bondman, on this hill.
MESSALA: Is not that he that lies upon the ground?
TITINIUS: He lies not like the living. O my heart!
MESSALA: Is not that he?

64 *Clouds* darkness and bad weather; *dews*, associated with night. Titinius is calling for all manner of disagreeable things to come upon them, because all their pleasure in life has departed at the death of Cassius.

65 *Mistrust of my success* fear of the result of my mission (line 15). 'Success' meant outcome, good or bad.

68 *apt* easily persuaded.

71 *the mother* the mind that conceives the error.

76 *envenomed* poisoned.

84 *misconstrued* misinterpreted.

85 Titinius places a laurel wreath, signifying victory, on Cassius.

86 *bid* bade.

88 *how I regarded* how highly I regarded, or honoured.

89 *By your leave, gods.* He is taking upon himself the responsibility of ending his life. *This is a Roman's part* this is the right thing for a Roman to do in this plight.

TITINIUS: No, this was he, Messala,
  But Cassius is no more. O setting sun,   60
  As in thy red rays thou dost sink to-night,
  So in his red blood Cassius' day is set.
  The sun of Rome is set. Our day is gone;
  Clouds, dews, and dangers come; our deeds are done.
  Mistrust of my success hath done this deed.   65
MESSALA: Mistrust of good success hath done this deed.
  O hateful error, melancholy's child,
  Why dost thou show to the apt thoughts of men
  The things that are not? O error, soon conceived,
  Thou never com'st unto a happy birth,   70
  But kill'st the mother that engendered thee!
TITINIUS: What, Pindarus! Where art thou, Pindarus?
MESSALA: Seek him, Titinius, whilst I go to meet
  The noble Brutus, thrusting this report
  Into his ears. I may say 'thrusting' it;   75
  For piercing steel and darts envenomed
  Shall be as welcome to the ears of Brutus
  As tidings of this sight.
TITINIUS: Hie you, Messala,
  And I will seek for Pindarus the while.   *Exit* MESSALA
  Why didst thou send me forth, brave Cassius?   80
  Did I not meet thy friends? And did not they
  Put on my brows this wreath of victory,
  And bid me give it thee? Didst thou not hear their shouts?
  Alas, thou hast misconstrued everything!
  But, hold thee—take this garland on thy brow;   85
  Thy Brutus bid me give it thee, and I
  Will do his bidding. Brutus, come apace,
  And see how I regarded Caius Cassius.
  By your leave, gods. This is a Roman's part.
  Come, Cassius' sword, and find Titinius' heart.   90
                                     Kills himself

The drawing opposite is of a battle scene from a film made in 1954: inevitably, it gives little idea of the wide field of action that can be shown in the cinema. Does *Julius Caesar* need realistic battle scenes?

94 A significant verdict on the situation. Cf. 2.1.167 and 3.1.270.

96 *proper*   own; it therefore emphasizes the idea—very own.

99 A simple but magnificent epitaph.
101 *fellow*   equal.
103 Another very moving line. It is a common experience that the full force of grief is not felt at the moment of bereavement, but wells up later, as though the immediate shock stuns the emotions. But Brutus was not permitted to find time.

Alarum. Re-enter MESSALA, *with* BRUTUS, *young* CATO,
LUCILIUS, LABEO, FLAVIUS, *and others*

BRUTUS: Where, where, Messala, doth his body lie?

MESSALA: Lo, yonder, and Titinius mourning it.

BRUTUS: Titinius' face is upward.

CATO: He is slain.

BRUTUS: O Julius Caesar, thou art mighty yet!
 Thy spirit walks abroad, and turns our swords   95
 In our own proper entrails.   *Low alarums*

CATO: Brave Titinius!
 Look whe'r he have not crowned dead Cassius!

BRUTUS: Are yet two Romans living such as these?
 The last of all the Romans, fare thee well!
 It is impossible that ever Rome   *100*
 Should breed thy fellow. Friends, I owe more tears
 To this dead man than you shall see me pay.
 I shall find time, Cassius, I shall find time.

104 *Thasos* an island off the coast of Thrace.

105 *funerals* funeral; funeral rites.

106 *discomfort* depress.

108 *set our battles on* advance our troops.

Another part of the field

Again we have the exceptional situation noted at the beginning of Scene 2.

2 *What bastard doth not?* who is so base that he does not?

4 Young Cato is therefore related to Brutus, who was both nephew and son-in-law of Marcus Cato. Cf. 2.1.295.

7 Lucilius takes up the defiant attitude of Cato. He claims to be Brutus in order to divert the enemy's attention from the real Brutus, and so both save Brutus and create confusion.

12 *Only I yield to die* I will yield by dying, but in no other way.

13 *There is so much.* He offers the soldier the honour of killing Brutus—i.e. the *so much* that he offers is explained by line 14.

16 *Room, ho!* make way there!

Come, therefore, and to Thasos send his body.
His funerals shall not be in our camp, *105*
Lest it discomfort us. Lucilius, come;
And come, young Cato; let us to the field.
Labeo and Flavius, set our battles on.
'T is three o'clock; and, Romans, yet ere night
We shall try fortune in a second fight. *Exeunt 110*

SCENE FOUR

Alarum. Enter BRUTUS, *young* CATO, LUCILIUS, *and others*

BRUTUS: Yet, countrymen, O, yet hold up your heads! *Exit*
CATO: What bastard doth not? Who will go with me?
I will proclaim my name about the field.
I am the son of Marcus Cato, ho!
A foe to tyrants, and my country's friend. *5*
I am the son of Marcus Cato, ho!
Enter Soldiers, *and fight*
LUCILIUS: And I am Brutus, Marcus Brutus, I!
Brutus, my country's friend; know me for Brutus!
CATO falls

O young and noble Cato, art thou down?
Why, now thou diest as bravely as Titinius; *10*
And mayst be honoured, being Cato's son.
FIRST SOLDIER: Yield, or thou diest.
LUCILIUS: Only I yield to die.
There is so much that thou wilt kill me straight;
Kill Brutus, and be honoured in his death.
FIRST SOLDIER: We must not. A noble prisoner. *15*
SECOND SOLDIER: Room, ho! Tell Antony, Brutus is ta'en.
FIRST SOLDIER: I'll tell the news. Here comes the general.

Enter ANTONY

Brutus is ta'en! Brutus is ta'en, my lord!

[·175·]

24 *or . . . or* either . . . or.

25 he will not be found in a dishonourable condition.

26 Antony is kind to the soldier—he does not gibe at his mistake. His clemency to Lucilius, and his compliment, show that he is anticipating victory, and wishes to ensure friendly relations all round after the fighting is over.

32 how everything has turned out.

Another part of the field

S.D. Brutus and his party straggle on, utterly weary, wounded and battle-stained.

2 Evidently Statilius had been sent out as a scout; he was to signal with a torch if his mission had succeeded.

15 *list* listen to.

ANTONY: Where is he?

LUCILIUS: Safe, Antony; Brutus is safe enough.   **20**
  I dare assure thee that no enemy
  Shall ever take alive the noble Brutus.
  The gods defend him from so great a shame!
  When you do find him, or alive or dead,
  He will be found like Brutus, like himself.   **25**

ANTONY: This is not Brutus, friend; but, I assure you,
  A prize no less in worth. Keep this man safe;
  Give him all kindness. I had rather have
  Such men my friends than enemies. Go on,
  And see whe'r Brutus be alive or dead;   **30**
  And bring us word onto Octavius' tent
  How everything is chanced.   *Exeunt*

SCENE FIVE

Enter BRUTUS, DARDANIUS, CLITUS, STRATO, *and*
VOLUMNIUS

BRUTUS: Come, poor remains of friends, rest on this rock.

CLITUS: Statilius showed the torch-light, but, my lord,
  He came not back. He is or ta'en or slain.

BRUTUS: Sit thee down, Clitus. Slaying is the word;
  It is a deed in fashion. Hark thee, Clitus.   *Whispers* **5**

CLITUS: What, I, my lord? No, not for all the world.

BRUTUS: Peace then. No words.

CLITUS: I'll rather kill myself.

BRUTUS: Hark thee, Dardanius.   *Whispers*

DARDANIUS: Shall I do such a deed?

CLITUS: O Dardanius!

DARDANIUS: O Clitus!   **10**

CLITUS: What ill request did Brutus make to thee?

DARDANIUS: To kill him, Clitus. Look, he meditates.

CLITUS: Now is that noble vessel full of grief,
  That it runs over even at his eyes.

BRUTUS: Come hither, good Volumnius; list a word.   **15**

22 *Thou seest the world ... how it goes* you see how affairs are shaping.

23 *the pit* the grave. It could also mean a pit into which animals were driven to be taken into captivity. Both meanings seem to apply, but Brutus' next remark can refer only to death.

27 *that our love of old* that old affection of ours.

29 *office* employment; task.

42 As a Stoic, Brutus sees death as the rest awarded to those who have toiled in life, though he departs from his Stoicism in committing suicide. Cf. 5.1.111.

45 *of a good respect* with a good reputation.

46 *smatch* smack, taste.

VOLUMNIUS: What says my lord?

BRUTUS: Why, this, Volumnius:
The ghost of Caesar hath appeared to me
Two several times by night—at Sardis once,
And, this last night, here in Philippi fields.
I know my hour is come.

VOLUMNIUS: Not so, my lord.   20

BRUTUS: Nay, I am sure it is, Volumnius.
Thou seest the world, Volumnius, how it goes;
Our enemies have beat us to the pit.   *Low alarum*
It is more worthy to leap in ourselves
Than tarry till they push us. Good Volumnius,   25
Thou knowest that we two went to school together;
Even for that our love of old, I prithee
Hold thou my sword-hilts whilst I run on it.

VOLUMNIUS: That's not an office for a friend, my lord.

Alarum louder

CLITUS: Fly, fly, my lord; there is no tarrying here.   30

BRUTUS: Farewell to you; and you; and you, Volumnius.
Strato, thou hast been all this while asleep;
Farewell to thee too, Strato. Countrymen,
My heart doth joy that yet in all my life
I found no man but he was true to me.   35
I shall have glory by this losing day
More than Octavius and Mark Antony
By this vile conquest shall attain unto.
So fare you well at once; for Brutus' tongue
Hath almost ended his life's history.   40
Night hangs upon mine eyes; my bones would rest,
That have but laboured to attain this hour.

Alarum. Cry within, 'Fly, fly, fly!'

CLITUS: Fly, my lord, fly!

BRUTUS: Hence! I will follow.

Exeunt CLITUS, DARDANIUS, and VOLUMNIUS

I prithee, Strato, stay thou by thy lord.
Thou art a fellow of a good respect;   45
Thy life hath had some smatch of honour in it.

50 *Caesar, now be still.* These words show that Brutus regarded his death as Caesar's revenge, which would enable the spirit of the murdered man to rest in peace. In Brutus' last moments, therefore, he admits that there is some ground for calling the killing of Caesar murder. Cf. also 3.2.43-4. Brutus admits defeat.

59 *Lucilius' saying.* Cf. 5.4.25.

60 *entertain* receive into my service.

61 *bestow* spend.

62 *prefer* recommend.

67 Messala takes the Roman view that suicide is noble when capture is the only alternative, therefore Strato has helped to preserve Brutus' nobility.

70 *that* that which, what.

71-2 he was the only one who joined the conspiracy on account of disinterested concern for the common people, anxious for the good of the community.

73 *gentle* noble; conducted according to high principle. *elements* humours, in the medieval sense. In the middle ages it was believed that four 'humours'—blood, choler, melancholy, phlegm—made up the human constitution, and both physical condition and character depended on a good balance of these. It was also believed that the natural world was made up of four elements—fire, earth, water, air—to which the humours corresponded, hence Shakespeare's interchange of the terms. He chooses *elements* here because he goes on to speak of *Nature*— Brutus was a masterpiece of Nature, perfectly proportioned in temperament.

75 '*This was a man!*' Again, a simple and utterly sufficient epitaph, a splendid echo of Brutus' own farewell to Cassius. Antony had said many bitter things about Brutus earlier, but Antony's feelings depended a good deal on circumstances. His love for Caesar coloured his attitude to Brutus at the time of Caesar's murder; the present occasion brings out his true opinion, which is penetrating enough to perceive the distinction between Brutus and the other conspirators. Also, he can now afford to be truthful.

Hold then my sword, and turn away thy face,
While I do run upon it. Wilt thou, Strato?
STRATO: Give me your hand first. Fare you well, my lord.
BRUTUS: Farewell, good Strato. Caesar, now be still;   *50*
I killed not thee with half so good a will.
Runs on his sword and dies

Alarum. Retreat. Enter OCTAVIUS, ANTONY, MESSALA,
LUCILIUS, *and the* Army

OCTAVIUS: What man is that?
MESSALA: My master's man. Strato, where is thy master?
STRATO: Free from the bondage you are in, Messala.
The conquerors can but make a fire of him;   *55*
For Brutus only overcame himself,
And no man else hath honour by his death.
LUCILIUS: So Brutus should be found. I thank thee, Brutus,
That thou hast proved Lucilius' saying true.
OCTAVIUS: All that served Brutus, I will entertain them.   *60*
Fellow, wilt thou bestow thy time with me?
STRATO: Ay, if Messala will prefer me to you.
OCTAVIUS: Do so, good Messala.
MESSALA: How died my master, Strato?
STRATO: I held the sword, and he did run on it.   *65*
MESSALA: Octavius, then take him to follow thee,
That did the latest service to my master.
ANTONY: This was the noblest Roman of them all.
All the conspirators save only he
Did that they did in envy of great Caesar;   *70*
He only in a general honest thought
And common good to all made one of them.
His life was gentle, and the elements
So mixed in him that Nature might stand up
And say to all the world, 'This was a man!'   *75*

The final scene in the Globe Theatre—Antony pays the last tribute to Brutus.

We first meet Brutus in 1.2. He reveals a good deal of his character in his conversation with Cassius: he declares he is not gamesome, and speaks disdainfully of Antony, who loves pleasure. He is a thinker, an idealist. We soon find that he has too much faith in people and assumes that they are more like himself than in fact they are. Despite his sarcasm about Antony, he trusts him to play fair at the funeral oration; he trusts too in the mob, never doubting that when he gives them the reasons for his action they will appreciate his motives. He trusts in the truth to prevail, and trusts people to pursue truth and not to be misled by emotion. He is a Stoic, and so believes in controlling his emotion by will-power. He manages this very well; he is not deficient in emotion—he is genuinely fond of both Caesar and Cassius, he profoundly loves Portia, he is unfailingly considerate to Lucius. But he is the person who quietens Cassius when Popilius makes the alarming remark before the murder, and he takes the terrible blow of Portia's death with wonderful fortitude. Having argued himself into assassinating Caesar he then tries to keep his hands clean, not really believing he has committed a crime at all; he has offered a sacrifice, which has cost him dear. On practical issues he constantly finds himself opposing Cassius: on the swearing of an oath; the advisability of killing Cicero and Antony; the wisdom of allowing Antony to speak at the funeral; the decision to fight at Philippi; leaving the favourable battle position. He is said to have given the word too soon in the battle—ironically, he did not, but the report does the damage. Ultimately he has to admit that he has failed; the very thing he tried to destroy, the spirit of Caesar, remains an active, effective force, and his philosophy has to give way under the stress of defeat—he cannot face captivity, and abandons the principles by which he has lived.

Many people consider the play to be 'The Tragedy of Brutus'. Do you think that would have been a better title? Would you rather side with Brutus and be beaten, or with Antony and be victorious? Or is it Julius Caesar who really triumphs after all?

76 *use* treat. The last words of the play are spoken by Octavius, the Caesar who is destined to assume the leadership of Rome Tyranny did not die in Act 3.

77 *rites* ceremonies.

79 *Most like a soldier* i.e. with all possible honour. *ordered honourably* richly arrayed.

80 *the field* the soldiers in the field.

81 *part* divide, share out. *happy* successful.

OCTAVIUS: According to his virtue let us use him,
With all respect and rites of burial.
Within my tent his bones to-night shall lie,
Most like a soldier, ordered honourably.
So call the field to rest, and let's away   80
To part the glories of this happy day.   *Exeunt*

INDEX TO NOTES

The abbreviation *pn* stands for the preliminary note preceding a scene and *an* stands for the after-note following a scene. References shown thus †114 refer to pages where the note is to a drawing.

READER'S NOTES